Abandoned in a Hammock

Abandoned in a Hammock

Hector M. Abreu

ISBN: 0692446982
ISBN 13: 9780692446980

Acknowledgements

I WOULD LIKE TO GIVE special thanks to Angel Rivera, Mike Valentino, Sara Klose and Bryan Gaul for their assistance and inspiration in helping me put my story into a book. This project would have never happened without your expertise and knowledge. I know that this book will help so many people and I am honored to have had all of you in my life to make this dream come true for me.

Dedication

❦

I WOULD LIKE TO DEDICATE this book to those who have been through the same kind of pain and mistreatment that I endured: child abuse, rape, molestation, verbal abuse, mental abuse, physical abuse, alcohol and drug abuse, and broken hearts. May this book bring you and your loved ones hope, happiness, freedom and joy. Your broken spirits can be healed! My hope is for you to be filled with sunshine by the time you have read my story.

Foreword

❧

PEOPLE WHO KNOW ME PERSONALLY have told me how amazed they are that I am so cheerful and optimistic – especially after they hear what my early life was like -- and that it can be described as "hellish." They say that having a personality such as mine, after such experiences, can be an inspiration, a victory of the human spirit. Well, I know I am not a hero. But this book is not meant only to tell my life story, but to explain when and where I reached decision points in my life, as to whether I'd become bitter and wicked – like many of the people around me growing up – or take a different course. I was only thinking about surviving at the time, of course, not about my actions' and choices' long-range implications, which may be instructive – even "inspirational" – to some other people. So here, with hopes that my perspective will benefit some readers in the midst of troubles like mine, or others who have faced similar problems but cannot see how to move beyond the pain, is my story. Writing it has released a great deal of suppressed pain for me, like black smoke confined in a burning house with close windows. May it rise to the heavens and turn into a rainbow.

Hector Manuel Abreu

Let's use bitter struggles as a springboard for development and change karma into mission! Let's transform all negative into positive value. Let's advance cheerfully. Daisaku Ikada.

CHAPTER 1

Puerto Rico, 1961

LEONOR HAD A HUNCH THINGS weren't quite right, so she hurried over to the ramshackle house. She heard the newborn screaming, right through the window, as insistent as a siren. "Iris, open up!" she shouted. No response. Leonor pounded her fists on the front door. Bam, bam, bam. No answer. Bam, bam, bam. "Iris! Iris!"

The west side window was loose, because Iris had never repaired it. Once Leonor remembered this, she swung back around and forced the window open. Leonor climbed in. She swept up the crying infant from his hammock. He was now nearly blue. She soothed him, holding a bottle of milk to his mouth as he hungrily sucked it down.

"That no good daughter of mine," Leonor muttered to herself. "Dancing the night away. Leaving her newborn alone in all evening, with a bottle propped up next to him. As if he can feed himself." Outside, the palm fronds whispered in the hot night. Leonor rocked her precious grandson until he fell asleep, his gnawing hunger alleviated. How would this child make it, with no mother to speak of? She closed her eyes and said a silent prayer.

That child was me, Hector Abreu, and this is my story.

Creamy white bows trimmed my first dress. I was a five-year-old boy, but my crazy cousin Julia wanted a girl. She slipped a burgundy velvet dress over my head -- the first of many dresses she had bought for me. White ruffled socks and little matching shoes adorned my feet. Julia added burgundy bows to my reddish auburn hair.

"There you go, Iris," she said. She called me "Iris," which was my mother's real name. My father had allowed Julia, a lovely but wild teenager, to move into our home so she could take care of me. Dad was busy carousing in the little towns that dotted Puerto Rico, enjoying a booze-filled lifestyle. He couldn't be bothered with me.

Julia had a boyfriend, whom no one in the family knew about. Puerto Rican families were strict back then, and did not allow young girls to date older men -- not to mention married men. Julia had told her married boyfriend that she had a daughter -- which was not true, of course. To keep the ruse going, she dressed me like little girl. I was so young that when I was dolled up like this, I actually looked -- and felt -- like a girl.

I met Julia's secret beau briefly, on his initial visit, when he showered me with puppets and dolls. He always entered and exited through the back door of the simple cement house. I don't remember what he looked like, because I'd only catch a glimpse of him as he snuck inside.

Julia would say she was "Mom" and her frequent male visitor was "Dad," and that we were going to play house. But they'd disappear to the back balcony instead, where they would make out. Then they'd usually slip into the bedroom. "He's sick," Julia would explain. So I'd park myself on the cool living room floor alone, amusing myself with dolls and teacups.

One time, Julia's secret lover surprised me with a little girl's dollhouse. It had pink walls and miniature sinks and tiny chairs, and my eyes lit up at the sight of it. I grabbed the toy house, fascinated with splendid gift. I plopped down in the middle of the living room in my burgundy dress, and began playing with my dolls. I flopped two dolls on the dollhouse couch, oblivious to the fact Julia and her lover had slipped into the human-sized bedroom. I arranged little plates and bowls in a circle on the kitchen table. I was so busy entertaining myself with my dollhouse, I didn't notice the exceptionally loud noises coming from the bedroom, where Julia and her boyfriend were apparently having acrobatic sex.

However, a neighbor noticed -- or rather, heard. She strolled over to make sure nothing was wrong. The lady peered through the screen door -- Julia had forgotten to close the front door that day -- and when she knocked, I answered. The neighbor was shocked to see me dressed like a little girl, because she knew I was a boy. I told her we were playing house, and "Mom" had to take care of "Dad" because he was sick, so they were in the other room. As the grunting and panting grew louder, the neighbor yelled for Julia to come out that instant.

Julia flew out of the bedroom and her secret lover bolted out the back door. My cousin grabbed me by the back of my dress and slammed the door in our neighbor's face. That was the end of Julia's babysitting for me.

My father was always looking for people to take care of me. But unfortunately, many of these relatives, like Julia, did not have my best interests at heart. My father's name was Angel Abreu, and he was a very handsome man, a player who cavorted with a different woman nearly every week. I remember him coming home in the finest cars, always with some beautiful lady. A heavy gambler, he disappeared for days, even weeks at a time, but he always brought me a new toy when he returned. I was the only kid on the block with the newest toys on the market -- not that it mattered much, since I never had anyone to play with. I was too afraid or shy to play with the neighborhood kids. At family gatherings, when I was expected to mix with other children, I would sit in a corner and entertain myself.

When I was a child, I had no idea what an "alcoholic" was, but I do remember how my father would come home reeking of booze. He'd be tired, grouchy, and to me, scary. His volatile mood swings terrified me to the point that when I heard him come through the front door, I'd crawl underneath the bed. If he found me, which he usually did, he would beat the crap out of me. He didn't seem to think he needed a reason. In his mind, I guess, being in a bad mood was enough justification. People would stare at my injuries -- bruises, black eyes, belt marks --with a questioning glance. Many times they would come right out and ask me if I was all right, and if anybody was hurting me. As a shy five-year old, trying to explain what was going on would have been even more traumatic than the beatings themselves. So I clammed up.

One time I was playing with a truck and fell into a hole. I got pretty banged up, including a black eye. The police were called, and they came and questioned my uncle, but nothing much came of it. That case really was an accident, but the point is that things were handled differently back then. Child abuse was not taken seriously, and kids like me suffered greatly because of this negligent attitude.

My parents had met when they were very young, and by all accounts they were just sex buddies. My mother's name was Juanita Iris Pagan. She and my father never married, and my mother left when I was so young that I don't even remember her. I don't know if she's still alive. I am told she used to walk around the Fernando Huncos Caserio housing project in short shorts and low-cut, revealing tank tops. Local women considered her the small town floozy, and shunned her. An exotic beauty, she had dark Indian skin, long black hair, a gorgeous face and a shapely body. I know this because as a teenager my favorite gay uncle, Uncle Manolin, described her to me.

My father first got my mother pregnant when she was 17. She gave birth to my brother Miguel Angel but then, probably scared and confused to have a baby when she was so young, she left the newborn on a hammock. She gave him a bottle of milk, came back three days later and found him dead. Everyone in town knew about it and hated her for it, especially my grandmother. I often wondered if it tore at my mother's heart to find her baby's lifeless body like that. Did she weep and wail? Or just shrug it off and get on with her life of partying and chasing men? I tend to believe it was the latter.

At age 19, she got pregnant again, this time with me. I was nearly blue when my grandmother found me, abandoned by my salsa-dancing mother. My grandmother Leonor whisked me off to her home and lovingly nurtured me back to health. She raised me until I was age five, when she passed away.

I vividly remember the day my grandmother died. The house was packed with family members and a crowd of people who were strangers to me. There was crying, screaming, wringing of hands. And tears. A lot of tears, because my grandmother was beloved in our community. People gravitated to her for her kindness, warm spirit, and welcoming attitude. I had no idea what was going on and why all those people filled our house that day. I just remember asking for Aguelita, which means Grandma in Spanish. They kept telling me that she was in the sky with God, and that He needed her so He wouldn't give her back. But at age five, I didn't understand. Since she was the only one who spoiled me and made me feel safe, I just wanted her back. For a long time, I kept crying and looking for her. Sometimes I think I'm still looking for her.

With my grandmother gone, there was nobody who genuinely wanted to take care of me. My father had no choice but to do it himself, in the best way he knew how -- which was not very well, frankly. Since he was rarely home, he left me with a series of babysitters, many of them relatives who were ill-equipped to watch a small child.

My first babysitter was my father's brother, Chuito. It was raining and thundering like crazy when my father dropped me off at my uncle's. The sky was so dark, it looked like night, even though it was morning. My uncle's place was downright spooky. I remember that his beat-up house was very small, and very filthy. The walls were a yellowish color, and clutter was haphazardly strewn everywhere.

Soon after I arrived, my uncle leaned down, looked me in the eyes and said, "Let's go to this room before the boogie man comes in. He hates kids, so I am going to protect you." At that moment I wasn't sure what I was more scared of, the "boogie man" or him. Uncle Chuito led me into his bedroom, a dingy little room with almost no furniture, just a bed and lots of junk. The bed was cheap and worn out, and the sheets were dirty and smelly. Outside the window, huge trees waved back and forth in the stiffening breeze. Through the torrential downpour, I could see lightning sizzle over the treetops. My uncle turned off the lights, threw me onto the stinky bed and climbed on top of me. I had trouble breathing as he pressed down on my small body. I remember he kept saying, "Now the boogie man won't steal you." He turned my head over to look at the window and told me that the boogie man was in the tree. My frightened eyes searched the dark skies but saw nothing. Thunder crashed and lightning lit up the room. Otherwise, there was only the sound of his increasingly rapid breathing. I became more petrified with each passing second.

Suddenly I felt a searing, agonizing pain. My uncle was penetrating me and whispering in my ear in a sickening voice that the boogie man was here. I screamed and cried, and tried to wrest myself away from this tall, thin man who felt so heavy on top of me. My pathetic struggling was futile, as I felt him repeatedly bouncing his body off of mine, thrusting his penis in deeper.

When he had his orgasm in me, I felt wet and fouled. My stomach heaved, and I wanted to vomit. Rolling over onto his side, my uncle panted and said, "Okay, you're safe now, the boogie man left." I buried my head in the pillow, refusing to look at him. "Don't tell anyone," he warned sternly, "or I'll have the boogie man come back and get you."

As Uncle Chuito cleaned me up in the bathroom, I choked back tears and wiped my non-stop running nose on my shirt-sleeve. I then huddled in a corner, traumatized, clutching my teddy mouse named Topo Gigio to my chest. It felt like

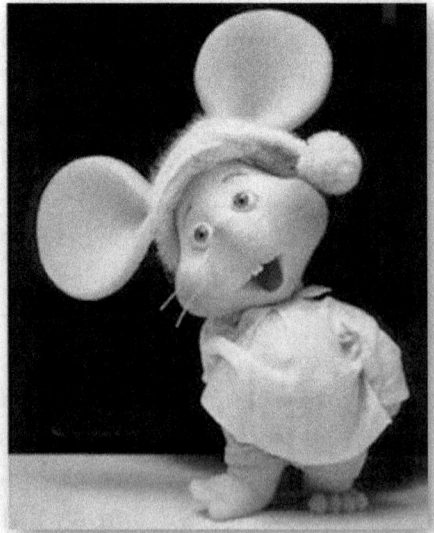

My Topo Gigio

long hours and days for me in that dank corner of that awful house. Finally, a beautiful lady arrived to pick me up -- one of my father's many girlfriends, but a stranger to me. She was the safety blanket I needed. I flung myself into her arms and wouldn't let go. Her voice was soft and kind, and she smelled like jasmine.

After this pretty lady took me home, I ran and hid underneath the bed. My Uncle Manolin was there. When my father returned home, drunk as usual, my uncle said I had hidden and refused to eat. My father dragged me out from under the bed, shoved me into a kitchen chair, and pushed a plate of food in front of me. I felt too sick to eat anything; it was like my stomach had closed up. My father was not the kind of man who would take no for an answer; he took the food and started shoving it down my throat. I was crying and choking on it. In frustration he threw down the spoon, and glared at me menacingly. He stalked off and fell into bed, exhausted from his latest drinking binge.

The next day, he was planning to take me back to Chuito's place. When we got close to the car, I started to scream and refused to get in. He yanked me toward the car door and demanded that I obey him. I kicked my legs and flailed my arms as he picked me up. He yelled that I was completely out of control. I was screaming, "No! No! No! The boogie man, the boogie man!" I remember crying while pointing to my bottom.

Then I saw a flash of recognition in my father's eyes. Suspicious now, he began asking me questions like what boogie man, where did he go? I just kept pointing to my bottom and crying hysterically. Finally he gave me a little pat on the head and said, "It's okay. It's okay, I won't take you to the boogie man."

Years later, my Uncle Manolin told me that as a result of this incident my father gave Chuito a savage beating with a baseball bat. It was his form of justice, and to some degree it is understandable given what had happened to me. I'm sure my father questioned his own judgment, because his brother had been in and out of hospitals and had serious mental issues. My father never used Chuito as a babysitter again – but I often wonder why he asked him to babysit me in the first place. Was my father simply uncaring? Or was his judgment impaired by his alcoholism? Or was he so desperate for women, he decided to pursue them without being hindered by a five-year-old? Or was it all of this? In any case, it was the height of irresponsibility, not to mention criminal endangerment of a child. I know people who wouldn't leave a pet with someone on anti-depressant pills, which suggests just how wrong my father's priorities were.

My new babysitter was my cousin, Joey, a young guy in his early twenties. When I was a teenager and already openly gay, my Uncle Manolin showed me a photo of Joey. I thought he was hot-looking, and as handsome as a model. But at age five, I lumped all grown-ups together, and, physical appearance didn't mean very much to me.

Joey spent most of his time sleeping and watching TV. I spent much of my time unsupervised in the house, even though Joey was supposedly babysitting me.

Lazy Joey did look to me to entertain him though. He would wake up from a nap and instruct me to lick his penis like a lollipop. I remember feeling his sperm dripping through my little fingers. He would say this was my private toy and no other little boy was allowed to play with it, so I'd better not tell anyone or he would take my toy away. He never penetrated me, he just had me play with my own private "toy." I barely understood any of this back then, of course.

One day while I was playing with my "toy," one of my father's girlfriends visited our house. She was looking for my dad, and while opening his bed-room door she spotted me and Joey "playing." When I saw her, I squeaked, "It's my toy, it's my toy." Joey started laughing, as if he really didn't care at all that he had been caught. I remember that the lady's body sort of reminded me of a guitar, and she had long thick hair and huge breasts. She quickly took me by the hand and led me away from Joey. She yanked up her blouse and showed me her gigantic breasts, with huge nipples.

She said, "You don't play with that; you play with these." I screamed, because it seemed like I had an alien looking at me with huge eyes. I can laugh about it now, but it didn't seem very funny to me back then.

Anyway, the lady dressed me and took me shopping. She treated me to ice cream too. Despite my initial scare at her huge naked chest, it did feel like she rescued me. She was my angel for the day. I never did see her again, but she must have said something to my dad, because the next day Joey was no longer my babysitter.

❧

But soon afterwards, my father took me to go live with Joey's mom, my Aunt Amelia, may she rest in peace. She lived in the town of Cantera. It may have been pretty at one time, but that was long before I lived there. My

I was seven in this picture

father had mentioned mango trees. I didn't see any mango trees in Cantera. What I recall is a small town of ramshackle houses, stranded on a peninsula at the edge of a dirty lagoon.

When my father had dropped me off at Aunt Amelia's, I couldn't understand why I was being passed off to yet another relative. So I was excited when she told me he was returning today. I would be going home, back to San Juan.

I'd spent the morning reading graffiti in the barrios, then chased after stray dogs. My aunt didn't like it when I roamed the dangerous streets, but I was a wild, disturbed child and hard to manage.

There were still hours to kill before my father's arrival, so in the afternoon, I picked through the garbage with Julia and Joey, two of Amelia's five children. Both humans and animals foraged for food in Cantera. The townspeople were as poor as slum dwellers in Rio.

Now I sat inside the little wood house, which balanced precariously on stilts made of garbage. I watched for my father through the open

shutters. Mosquitoes dive-bombed me. Bugs skittered across the wooden floor. There was filth all around me, and the smell of refuse was overpowering. One good thing came from my time in that pig-sty: to this day, I am a stickler for neatness, cleanliness and order.

Then I saw it. A silver Ford Falcon. It had to be his. My father liked to gamble and drink, and often wheeled around in fancy automobiles. As he approached the house, I saw the vehicle slow in the muck left from yesterday's rainstorm. It didn't matter to me if the wheels of his beautiful new auto were coated with mud. We were going home, such as it was.

I clutched my teddy bear and the toy cars he had bought me when he left me with Amelia four months ago. My favorite blue T-shirt, hand-sewed by my aunt, rested on the kitchen table along with my folded shorts and tops.

My father got out of the car, a cigar dangling between his lips. A lovely lady -- one of his many girlfriends -- linked arms with him, and they strolled to the front door. I dashed to him. "Papa!" I yelled. He handed me a toy tugboat, and called for my aunt. He handed her a wad of cash, and whispered something I couldn't make out. "Thank you" or "Is that enough?" I'll never know.

Amelia served us chicken, rice and pinto beans; it was about all she could afford, and practically all we ate while I lived there. A mere ten minutes later, my father and his dark-skinned lady headed to the car. "No! No! Papa!" I shouted. "Take me with, take me with you." But my aunt held me as the Ford slid away. I wrangled free, and hurled my new toy boat out the window. I watched it sail down, spinning in circles, its blue hull twisting and turning until it stuck in the clay mud, right next to yesterday's cans of beans and paper bag rice.

Okay, back to Aunt Amelia. If nothing else, she was a survivor. She did whatever she needed to keep her five children from going hungry, since she was a single mom, and I must add a wonderful woman who was good to everyone. I remember walking alone on her street. I saw things as a five year old kid that most adults haven't seen in this lifetime -- prostitutes, gang members, people being shot, riots, drug usage – you name it I saw it. Luckily, I never got hurt or bothered by anyone since the neighbors knew that the Abreus were a bit nuts, so no one dared to touch us.

But what I haven't been able to understand, even to this day, was why in the hell my father took me to live with Aunt Amelia. She was Julia and Joey's mother, and they lived in the house with her! So of course, I got my live Joey "toy" back for a few months when there was often no one around for long stretches of the day but just him and myself.

Julia never dressed me up like a girl again and she was actually nice to me when I went to live there. Who knows - maybe she felt sorry for me. I do know Amelia would let her kids get away with murder; they had no respect for her or anyone. She was wonderful, but a little crazy – loca. If you messed with her or her family, she would run after you with a bat and crack your head open and not look back! My family had little formal education, which might explain why they never took me to a therapist when I got raped and abused sexually and mentally. Gosh, I sometimes wonder how I survived all this at such a young age.

My father used to come by once in a while for maybe five minutes, to give his sister Amelia money and say hello to me. But then he came by less and less and, since Amelia couldn't afford to support me, she had to take me to the country so my other aunt, Aunt Petra, could mind me.

Aunt Petra had a cement house and a lot of land. She also had a husband and five kids and was in a better situation, in terms of money and housing, than Aunt Amelia. So my Aunt Petra was my next babysitter, along with six other members of her family. My aunt had chores for all her kids, just as in most families. These were things like helping out around the house or maybe running down to the corner store or some other errand. The bottom line was, they were being taught responsibility. I had never been given chores or told to do my homework, so all of this was new to me. Not to mention, by the time I went to live with them for three months I was already a very disturbed child.

So I resisted her attempts to teach me to be helpful and cooperative. I'm ashamed to say it now, but I was bratty, and would constantly fight her about anything she asked me to do. But looking back on those days, her discipline was the best thing for me at that time, in any number of ways. I have to thank her for helping me with so many of the things that I needed to know to get along in this world. I learned how to take a bath, brush my teeth, comb my hair, put my clothes away on hangers, and how to make myself a sandwich. These activities might not sound like much, but they are important everyday skills for a kid who never had anybody around to teach him the practicalities of life.

Her kids and I would get into fights over just about anything. Of course, as usually happens with kids, we'd soon end up playing together again. However, on occasion they would be a bit brutal with me. I remember one day they coerced me into jumping from the roof of the house onto a small hill that rose up behind it, which would get very muddy and slippery when it rained. They told me that if I jumped from the roof onto the hill that I would be more like their brother. My heart thumping in my chest, I swallowed hard and agreed to do it. I wanted so badly to fit in!

One of the kids dragged over a rickety old ladder he'd found somewhere, and leaned it up against the house. I slowly scanned their grinning faces as they jeered and dared me to start climbing. With much trepidation, I grabbed hold of one of the ladder's rusty rungs and began to pull myself up. With each step I was getting higher off the ground—and perilously closer, it seemed, to certain doom. I kept staring up toward that intimidating roof, too scared to look back down. Finally I reached the top and gingerly clambered onto the roof.

Still afraid to look down, I could hear the kids far below whistling and cheering. "Jump! Jump! Jump!" came the chant. Or was it more of a taunt? Bending low, my knees nearly touching the asphalt shingles, I made my way to the far side of the roof, nearest to the hill. The hot sun was beating down on me and I had to keep wiping the sweat off of my forehead as it dripped into my eyes, stinging them with its bitterness.

At that moment, I wanted nothing more than to just scurry back to the ladder and climb back down to the safety of the ground, but I knew I would never live down the kids' cruel insults if I did. They would tease me more mercilessly than ever.

So, gathering up my courage, I stood up tall, took in a deep breath and leaped off that confounded roof. My small body hurtled into space, seemingly suspended in mid-air for a nanosecond, and then gravity took over and pulled me onto the hillside. Crashing to the earth with a thud, I instinctively curled my body into a ball and rolled down the steep incline to where there was a small, muddy creek. I got pretty banged up and filthy from the red clay, and I earned nothing but a huge bump on my head for my foolish stunt, which I naively thought would make me look courageous. The kids were all laughing hysterically at me, while I was crying and terrified. My aunt was furious when she found out what had happened, and she harshly punished all of us.

She was also angry because we were all dressed up to go to church that day, and I was wearing all white clothing. After that fall, I looked like I'd been rolling in a pigpen. To make matters even worse, my father showed up. Up to that point, he had no idea that my Aunt Amelia had taken me to live with Petra, since he wasn't around to know what was up with me.

His solution for my dirtied white clothes? He just started beating me, because supposedly I had misbehaved and hadn't been a "good little boy" for my Aunt Petra. Thankfully, my aunt eventually got in the way and stopped him and had him take me to the hospital to make sure I was not injured. This was one of those few moments I felt that maybe I was special in my father's eyes, and thought he was there to bring me home. Looking back on it now, however, I'm all but certain that he took me to the hospital primarily to look good in front of the family.

My father gave Aunt Petra some money, then left and didn't return for a few months. By this time, my aunt had started to notice that I was always looking down at her boys' private parts and caught me playing with them a few times. After that she wouldn't let me near her boys! Enraged, she isolated me from them and made me sleep in the dining room on a small fold up mattress. Today, in the twenty-first century, her attitude would be called homophobia and it is a real fear. She also gave me a (relatively tame) beating and told me that boys don't touch other boys.

I could tell that she felt uncomfortable having me there after that, so she tried getting in touch with my father. That, of course, proved to be impossible since neither she, nor anyone else for that matter, really ever knew where he was or what he was up to. So she packed my bag and dropped me off at my father's. I was once again unwanted – a lost boy with nobody to turn to.

Every adversity, every failure, every heartbreak, carries with it the seed of an equal or greater benefit."

Napoleon Hill.

CHAPTER 2

❦

WHILE I WAS STILL FIVE years old, my Cousin David had moved in to stay at my family's house back in the city. He was a young guy in his twenties, and my Aunt Petra would just drop me with him, saying, "Here, I can't take care of him," then simply left. Of course, she never knew back then that I already had been raped by her brother Chuito, molested by her nephew Joey, and dressed up like a little girl by her niece Julia. No one ever told her anything.

But Cousin David did know all, about it. I don't know how he knew, but my guess is that my Uncle Manolin had mentioned it to him, since he lived in the same house with my father and me. My uncle was never around. He would sleep during the day, and worked as a security guard at night, so he wasn't much of a factor in my life at that time.

David was a very nice guy, and from my recollection he was trying to make me become a regular little boy. So he did things with me that boys would usually do, baseball, basketball, and play with all the "guy" toys I had in the house.

One day, he and I were playing basketball, and the ball rolled into the street. He yelled to me to, "Go get the ball," so I ran into the middle of the street and BAM! I got hit by a car on my right side. I was stunned, shocked, my head was ringing and my ear hurting badly. Traffic stopped, and people were standing around. I heard a kind of murmuring, as if the spectators were far away from me, asking me if I was all right.

I thought I was. My bruises were painful, but the car didn't hit me very hard, so that there was no blood or broken bones or anything like that. Basically, the car didn't strike me, but rather, I bounced off of it. So David figured I didn't need a hospital - he probably didn't want the responsibility either.

He cradled me in his arms as I was crying, comforted me and nurtured me like a big brother. My whole right side hurt for a long time. He really didn't bother telling anyone because, I guess, he didn't want to get in trouble. And me being just five years old he thought everything was going to be okay.

But because he didn't tell our family about my accident, I didn't get checked out by a doctor. The truth was that I had an ear injury that needed to be treated, but wasn't. As a result, I suffered from ear infections until I was almost 21 years old.

Later in life, I was to learn that the ear is a highly delicate part of the body, and to neglect treating it was not wise. I remember those years as awful, with puss constantly oozing out from my ear. The pain at times was unbearable, so bad that when I became a teenager and unable to sleep due to the pain, I used to walk around the streets in the middle of the night, desperate for relief and sobbing aloud in agony. It felt like someone took a screwdriver and was just digging it deeper and deeper into my ear -- over and over! No matter what the doctor, gave me it just would not go away and would get even worse at times.

I eventually had three ear surgeries, two in Chicago when my father brought me there to live, and another one more in Puerto Rico when I moved back there from Chicago.

To leap ahead about 10 years (because it relates to this injury I suffered as a child), I had my first "puppy love" boyfriend when I was around 17 years old, and he used to stay up taking care of me for hours into the middle of the night. It was wonderful to feel loved and cared about. He was going to college, working full time and his job gave him a great insurance plan. He put me down as his brother so I could be covered too.

After being with him for around three years, he took me to an ear doctor who gave me my third surgery and wow. Heaven! I was pain-free and puss-free for the first time since I was five. What indescribable relief.

Goosebumps are springing up as I'm writing this, and I'm choking up inside as I reflect back on the day of that surgery. I remember all my gay friends coming to the hospital to cheer me up when I was all bandaged up and recuperating. It felt really good having them there, like I wasn't alone in the world.

My only other entertainment in the hospital was watching TV, because I was still in some pain from the surgery and couldn't really move much. One day, a tall male nurse walked in to check on me. He started chatting with me and soon realized that I was gay. He asked me if needed anything, and to make his point he was rubbing his cock in his tight nurse uniform. I asked him if he could help me reach the hospital phone. I was reaching for the phone, he pressed his hard penis against my hand so I could play with it. He asked me to pull his zipper down, then closed the hospital curtain and took out his penis. I was already familiar with all this, so I knew what was coming next; sure enough, he had me go down on him.

Then he asked me if I needed help taking a shower. He helped me into the shower and started bathing me but then told me to turn around, and penetrated me (though at least he was gentler than my rapist uncle). But once he had his orgasm, he withdrew, pulled his pants up and warned me to never even think of telling anyone about it. The most hurtful part was that he said all this in a very menacing tone, with an evil look in his eyes, then left me there to finish my shower myself.

At this point in my life, when this type of thing happened to me, I thought of it as normal, since I had already been sexually exploited so many times before. More about all of this in later chapters.

But coming back to my story when I was five years old, my life became a roller coaster. I lived in so many homes and with so many people I didn't even know where to call home – or who to call Mom.

Every time my father got a new girlfriend, he would move us in with her. He would stay maybe a week to several months with most of them, but he would always leave me there with the girlfriend, and disappear for days or weeks. Many of these beautiful ladies, needless to say, were ticked off at him and got frustrated to have to take care of a child who didn't belong to them. Being mad at my father, they would take it out on me and treat me very harshly. And when they realized that he wasn't coming back for me, they would pack my stuff and drop me off at the front of our house and just drive away. Only a few of them used it as an excuse to see if they would run into my father, since most of them were madly in love with him. His usual practice was to just dump them, leave me with them, and disappear.

By the time I was seven or eight, I already knew how to take care of myself pretty well, thanks to my Aunt Petra. I could cook a little, do my laundry, get ready for school and pack my own lunch. I would walk to school by myself, and get home by myself. I hardly ever did homework, since there was nobody there to make sure I did it. As a result, I did so poorly in school that my report cards showed nothing but F's – except just one A, for Art.

Art for me was therapy and it remains so today. So when my father would get the report card and saw all the F's, he would beat the daylights out of me. I used to go to school with black eyes and bruises many times, and since I was a very shy and scared kid I never told anyone about it. I always would sit in back of the class, hiding, hoping not to be noticed. My father never bothered to help me with schoolwork, but perversely, expected me to have good grades.

This went on for a few years. When I turned eight, I was already a very independent kid, all I needed was a job and my own apartment. Around this time, my father had supposedly fallen in love with a "lady" named Dolores. Of course, she was a very beautiful woman like all the others, and had two kids of her own, Junior and Enrique, who were a few years younger than me – just toddlers, really.

For reasons that will become painfully obvious later, I will point out here that – ominously - "Dolores" means "sorrows" in Latin, and this awful woman would eventually cost me enough sorrow for any lifetime – and by age 8, I had already had more than my share.

To return to my narrative, my father had met Dolores in San Lorenzo, a little town in the middle of nowhere, in Puerto Rico. Although a very tropical and beautiful place, it was dirt poor, the houses all made of wood, with tin roofs. The area was very hilly with small creeks and gigantic rocks surrounded by trees, and there were all kinds of animals in the forest. Other than the terrible poverty, it was a quaint, pretty area. The people of the town were very kind, giving, loving and religious people.

A few of my cousins lived in this town, where my dad met Dolores. She lived across the dirt road on top of a hill, in a wooden house with steel rooftop and shuttered windows. She lived there with her two children, her parents, and her brother. It was a small house, and constantly hot and stuffy because the sun would always be beating on the steel roof. When it rained you could hear it pounding like thunder on top. In their kitchen, the sink was a tub on stilts outside the window, and this is where they washed dishes. I remember when you would wash dishes, you could glance down the hill and see all the rusted, dilapidated little homes layering the slope all the way to the bottom.

Still, it all looked so beautiful! And beyond the sink, the water ran down a pretty little creek surrounded by trees and bamboo. There were lots of colorful flowers and the most gorgeous trees, called Flanboyan. It was a glorious, bucolic setting where Nature reigned. There were horses, cows, pig, chickens, goats, roosters. It was like a wildlife refuge. But this beautiful place didn't make me any Tom Sawyer - not in the stage of life I was in at that time.

But its natural splendor notwithstanding, the place was primitive. The toilet facilities were Stone Age, an outhouse latrine right next to the creek and a few feet from the house and beside the shower. In the outhouse was a simple board with a hole cut in it. Every once in a while, somebody would pour lime down the hole, but usually it was horribly smelly and bug infested. Oh my God! I had never used a latrine before and was so disgusted. After all, I was a city boy, used to actual toilets; even my Aunt Amelia had a toilet in her poor, tiny house.

When in there, you would get eaten alive by mosquitoes while using the toilet, and there were huge flies everywhere, drawn by the human waste. Also, the outhouse sat in an unshaded spot and was usually hot as hell. Every minute spent in there was pure torture, including the need to constantly swat insects to keep from being eaten alive. You could see all the waste at the bottom of this hole. It was nasty!

So, getting back to how I ended up in San Lorenzo, my father had moved in with Dolores after only a month, and you can just imagine how crowded it was, with eight people living in a tiny, two bedroom, small living room house.

When my father moved in with her, I didn't think much about it, because he had done it so many times before, by this time I thought it was just a normal thing to do. At the beginning, it was all-good with Dolores pretending to be a good stepmother in front of my father. Well, she ended up being the step mom from Hell! While she was very good to her own kids, she was terrible to me. She treated me like I was some sort of wild animal. At this point in life, I wasn't just tolerating abuse from Dad's girlfriends, so I did defend myself. I was only eight, but was almost like an adult, kind of a man-child, by virtue of my hard life. Whatever she did to me I would do right back to her; and so we became enemies. She hit me, and I hit her; she spit on me, and I spit on her; she pulled my hair, and I pulled hers. Estel, her mother, felt sorry for me, so she would always step between us and protect me. After all, it was a kid against an adult. I must say that, no matter what happened to me, I always had some type of a guardian angel come to my rescue, whether it was a strange woman or a female family member, which explains why, even to this day, I feel so comfortable around women, more than men. They are less threatening, and generally are more nurturing than men.

Getting back to Miss Dolores; things got so bad at her place that I spent most of my time across the road with the cousins till my father came home. My cousin Martha was really nice to me, teaching me many things like household chores, which I became better - at even though I already knew how to do many of them. She would spend hours with me and again, like most women, was a real friend to me.

My cousin Tono would also hang out and play with me. We had no toys there, since mine were left in our house in the city. So we used to climb trees, go hiking, catch pigeons, kill, clean, cook and eat them. They were sort of tasty, and their flavor was all new to me. It was so cool to climb a tree, look down the hill and see all the beautiful mountains. We spent hours up there in those trees. We took really long walks, often going into barns and meeting all kinds of strange people, including travelers just passing through, along with some bums and druggies.

My cousin was good as a leader. I was always just a follower, and would let him be the guide, and just walked behind him. I was always too shy to speak to anyone, and also very afraid of people.

One thing though, I was always waiting for that moment when we were supposed to have sex, since that had already happened to me so often. But this time, I was just being a boy with another boy.

I got to see him after many years and he really wasn't too friendly to me. He wasn't unfriendly, he did chat with me and talk about the old times up in the tree, and he sure did talk about his girlfriend a lot! I got the feeling that it was very important to him to let me know that he was not gay. I couldn't really figure it out. Well, he did turn out to be a very handsome man, and it seemed like he was sweet, and treated women very well. I guess his droning on about his lady was a way for straight men to distance themselves from anyone they perceived as gay, especially in the macho Latino culture.

My cousin's father used to raise and kill pigs for a living. I remember the family all used to get up at six in the morning to kill the pigs while I stood there and watched them. Martha and other family members would start cleaning up after the process; she and my cousin Tono were teaching me how it was done. It was all revolting to me, but I'd rather watch a pig get slaughtered and butchered than be home with Dolores.

The butchering chamber was a very poor, middle-sized room that had no walls, just a steel roof on posts, between four big tree trunks that served as walls, and situated deep in the forest. There was a huge sink beside a big dirty old table, on which they cut up the pigs and cleaned the carcasses. I can just smell the blood like it was yesterday, a kind of copper, awful smell. And I can still hear the pigs squealing while they were being killed. They would tie the pig up by the back feet, and hang him from a tree branch, slit his throat with a huge knife, then drain his blood - which gushed out like water from a faucet for a while.

Poor things. Somehow, my sense of justice was offended by slaughtering defenseless animals.

After they were done with the preparation, they would roast the pig in their front yard for hours. Eventually, the smell of blood disappeared and the wonderful, tantalizing aroma of roasted pork filled the little town. It smelled so good, and tasted amazing!

Around two o'clock or so in the afternoon, customers would start coming over to buy the delicious meat. This happened every Saturday like clockwork.

I also remember that behind the house there was a little dirt road that spiraled down to the street and would lead us to the town's main street. We would go to the little local bodega, a tiny store, to buy candy and anything needed for the house.

I remember coming back up the spiral road one day, and telling my cousin Tono that I had learned that little boys can have babies. I don't know why I was telling him this. I guess I was looking for some type of answer, since I had been molested so many times, and already knew where babies came from. So I was making it up. It was some sort of fantasy of mine, and having to do with my confusion about sex. I was never taught anything about sex or life, and was left to draw my own conclusions.

I was so confused about sex. As I was telling Tono this, a teenage boy from down the hill heard me talking, and just looked at me and smiled - like he knew I was a little gay boy (I was also very effeminate). At the time, I didn't think anything of that incident, but it would turn out to be very important later.

That same day my uncle had bought a new refrigerator, which, in those days, would come in a box as big as the fridge itself. So my cousin Tono and I took the huge box and turned it into a little store; cut out a "window" on its front, and put sticks on each corner to prop the window up, and so we could open and close it. Then we took the very little money we had from helping my uncle slaughter the pigs, went to the corner store and bought a lot of candy which we tacked up with thumbtacks so it looked like a store, and poof, we were in business. We put the box on the corner behind my uncle's house, right where the spiral hill started. It was somewhat out of the way since not too many people really went back there, and was surrounded by trees.

We didn't sell a thing, and just ate most of the candy. But later that day, Tono had to go home and I stayed alone at the box store, pretending I was a storeowner. Then the teenager who had smiled knowingly at me earlier that day came back up the hill, and stopped and asked me what I was doing. I can't remember what my answer was, but I did ask him if he wanted to buy candy.

We just had a pieces few left, so this tall, handsome stranger with very black hair asked me if he could go inside to pick the candy, and I let him. He started playing with his penis under his pants, and of course I started to look and kind of knew what was coming (so to speak). He asked me if I wanted to play with his "candy," and then took his penis out. He had me suck him, then closed the box door window and proceeded to penetrate me. After pulling his pants up, he just walked away. He didn't say anything to me or threaten me, and for me, well, such an experience was just a normal thing. I didn't think anything of it. I never told anyone anything about it, since I'd been molested so many times, then ordered not to say anything about it. I just thought that every time it happened, I had to keep it a secret.

Right after that, it started raining. The box got all shriveled up and I went home to Dolores's house like nothing had ever happened. Estel sat me at the table, served me dinner, and that was that. It was as though being used sexually was nothing out of the ordinary.

By this time, I was already enrolled in school, which was somewhat of a ride away, roughly one mile. The school enclosed a big open space, surrounded with tiny houses that were the classrooms, maybe ten of them or so, all this set against a backdrop of jungle, mountains and a river.

I remember how hot it was in that school, and that sitting in the classroom was like being in a sauna. The windows were kept open, fans going full blast, but we were still sweating like dogs even the teacher. I didn't really speak to anyone, just sat in back of the class, again hoping no one would notice me. The teacher would ask me questions and I never knew how to answer them, so I started shaking and got dreadfully nervous. I just held still in class saying nothing, waiting anxiously for art class, and time to go home.

Recess became one of my especially scary times. In some way that I can't remember, I started hanging out with a few of the boys. We really didn't play, they would just push me around like I was a punching bag and I wouldn't object.

One day, they asked me to go with them down to the river behind the school. There were three or four boys in this group, and their pleasure was to have fun with me. Their "fun" on this occasion was that they threw me down the hill that was covered with bamboo and heavy brush and jungle. When I say they pushed me I mean that all of them at the same time picked me up and flung me down the hill. It was a terrible feeling of having no control and feeling myself flying down the hill. I went head over heels crashing through the bamboo trees and tearing through the brush.

Finally, I landed, numb, at the bottom in the mud and on the edge or the river. When I got up and took a look at myself, I was all bruised and scratched and dirty from the mud. I was still stunned and when I looked up to see where the howling laughing sounds were coming from, there they were, my tormentors. They were just laughing really hard and rather than defending myself, I just stood there bawling like a little sissy.

When it came time to go back to class, the teacher looked at me and asked me what happened. I was so scared I wouldn't even look at those boys, and instead, told her that I slipped while playing by the river. What a mistake that was! Now sure that I wasn't going to rat them out to the teacher, they considered me a real juicy target. After that, those kids became even more evil to me. I was their pansy, their punching bag, always good for a few laughs.

My way of handling school and recess was to spend lots of time alone sitting somewhere till it was time to go back to class, those ten minutes feeling like ten hours for me. Finally each day, the bell rang and it was time to go home. I flew out of my seat and ran to wait for the bus.

Then, in order for me to get to the Dolores monster's house, after getting dropped off by the bus I had to walk right by the front of this bar and pool place my father had opened up, and where he spent all of his time. I tried to run past the place, but he saw me and called, "Hector! Get over here, what happened to you?"

I just looked at him with fear-filled eyes, afraid to tell him, and so I repeated the same story I'd told the teacher, then walked away.

I definitely didn't want to hurry back to Dolores's place, so on my way home, I used to stop by this little hiding place I found in the forest. There was a peaceful murmuring creek nearby, where I used to play by myself.

I sometimes would lay in the grass, gaze up into the sky and imagine what animals and things the passing clouds looked like. Always I would plead to my grandma, as I sobbed, deeply hurt. "Grandma," I prayed, *"Why did you leave me? Please take me with you. Why are these things happening to me? I don't understand. Please take me home. Help me. Tell me what to do. Where is my mom? Why isn't she coming to get me? Why is everyone so mean to me? Please send me a sign. Tell me something. Ask God why He is doing this to me."*

This lingering and daydreaming was my escape hatch, my haven. While it was a blessed relief and a form of therapy, it did get me in trouble, because my family would always ask me where the hell I had been, since I was supposed to be home by three.

I really started to be afraid of going back to school, so the family would get me ready to go. Well, Estel did; Dolores couldn't care less, and I would leave out the door and hide behind the trees and bushes around a huge rock to try to avoid school. I did this many times, till they figured it out, and I got a good beating for it. Dolores loved it when my father used to beat the crap out of me.

One day, I slipped on a rock and bent my foot really bad, so bad that I couldn't walk for weeks. The following day I stayed there hiding in considerable pain till I heard the school bus pass by, and I knew it was time to go home. I walked to the house, and Estel took care of me right away when she saw me limping. They didn't take me to a medical doctor, but to a witch doctor who lived nearby to try to heal my foot.

That "treatment" was so weird and scary. This man put some sort of mixture on my foot, then started slapping it with a palm frond. He was an old man, really wrinkly, with a long beard and grayish hair, and he kept babbling nonsensical chants and spells. To say the least, it was a truly bizarre experience, and I would have greatly preferred a regular MD, thank you very much.

After that, I had to stay home for a few weeks since I couldn't walk. I was in heaven since I didn't have to go through the torments of school, and yet in hell having to be around Dolores all the time. But somehow I dragged myself across the dirt road to my cousin's house, where I spent most of my two weeks. I used to beg my father to please let me stay with them as a sleepover, and most of the time he didn't really care since it was only across the road, and he was always at the bar; not even Dolores got to see him that much.

One of the things that I remember most vividly from those days was how my father and Dolores would constantly fight like cats and dogs. She would tell him that she hated that "fucking bar," and threatened that she would have someone burn it down. So in order for her to be around him, she started hanging out at the bar almost every night, which made things worse because she would see all the ladies flirting with him (remember, he was very handsome). I used to love it when they fought. I kept thinking that eventually they would break up, and Dad and I would go back home to the city. But strangely, it didn't happen. Somehow, she really had some control over him.

She was so controlling and such a bitch, whom I hated as much as she hated me. One Sunday, Estel couldn't baby-sit because she went to church with all the older ladies from the town. Also my family from across the road. They went to the only mass served that day. Dolores wasn't a church type of girl, so I had to stay with her and her two boys.

She told me and her boys to go outside and play cowboys and Indians. Well, guess who was the Indian? (aka, "victim") She told her sons to tie me up to a tree next to the house, while she sat in the living room from which she could watch this whole spectacle. She ordered Enrique to take a tree branch and to whip my feet; it hurt like hell, and she laughed like the sadistic trash she was.

At that point I knew I was in serious trouble due to one of her many evil tricks. She told her other son to open the gate that penned some goats up, then to push them towards me. These goats had horns and were not only unfriendly, but downright nasty. While the goats were getting loose, and I was screaming, "Let me go! Let me go!" She handed her son Junior a huge knife -- and calmly told him to stab me.

So Junior, being a little kid, did what his mother was telling him, and took the knife and slashed me with it across the eyes and nose. So there I was, tied up to a tree, one son whipping me with branches, Junior hacking across my nose, and the goats turned loose to ram me. When Junior jabbed me, blood rushed out of my nose like an open water hose. That cruel bitch Dolores was laughing her ass off, while her kids (who had the excuse of being too young to know any better) were jumping, laughing and whooping like cowboys while I was tied to the tree, screaming, crying, and completely hysterical.

Luckily for me, my father had forgotten something at home and returned to pick it up, when he saw me tied up, bleeding and howling he began yelling, "What the hell is going on here!" He started untying me, pressing a rag on my nose, and eventually rushed me to the hospital. I had three stitches and came home with a swollen nose all bandaged up. I still bear the scars – both physical and emotional – of this incident of diabolical cruelty.

This was the first time my father saw her being brutal to me, since he never believed me about the other things she did to me. He thought I was just a kid making up dreadful lies because I hated my stepmother. He was right about that part though, I truly did hate her.

But she got caught in the act, because Dad got to see her laughing while she was sitting in the living room, watching and enjoying my torment. When she noticed that he was back, the bitch tried to put on a good show, jumped up and yelled at her kids, "What are you doing? Get inside the house, you boys are going to be punished!"

But it was too late, my dad had already seen it all. I thought that after this he would take me back home to the city. Yet, incredibly, he didn't do a thing about the atrocity he had seen with his own eyes! He just took me back to Dolores.

They had a tiny fight, but then he went back to work at the bar, and that evil woman gave me this terrifying look that said, "If you value your life, you won't cross me, brat!" That night, she didn't let me sleep in the bedroom, because she feared I would retaliate at her somehow, if I could get near her. So she made me sleep on a hammock in the living room. In the middle of the night I fell out of it, right on my face onto a hard cold cement floor. Oh my God, did that hurt! I started crying quietly in the dark, but Estel heard me, came to the living room and found me there covered with blood and sobbing in a corner. She cleaned me up and took me to sleep with her in her room in her little bed.

This all happened about one in the morning or so. Dolores heard the commotion and screamed, "What the hell is wrong with him now? Make him go to sleep and stop disturbing us. I need my beauty sleep."

Estel really got on her ass for doing this to me, but Dolores was a spoiled she-devil who never respected her mother, and never listened to her.

Around this time, my father started building a cement house just behind her old wooden one. The bar was making money and the she-monster wanted a new house, so my father built her one (and pretty fast, I might add). It was a small three-bedroom structure, with a beautiful view of the hill and mountains.

Not long after we moved in there, a new face appeared – a new menace. It was Tito, her brother who was in the army and looked just like her, almost like twins. Dolores would tell Tito all sorts of crap about me, what a terrible kid I was, that I didn't respect her (she was right about that), that I would beat up her kids, pull her hair, spit at her and so on. All of which was true, because I had to defend myself since no one else did, except her mother, the sweet Estel. Also, Tito must have noticed that I was gay since I was so feminine, even though I didn't know that myself at the time.

Unfortunately, he was just as horrible as she was! He started ordering me around to do this and that for him. I would refuse to, so he started calling me a "fucking little faggot!" Then he'd taunt me, saying, "You are a faggot aren't you?" He would knock me over my head with his knuckles and that hurt. He would tell me, "Hey you, faggot, if I ever find you touching my sister or her kids, I am going to fucking beat you up!"

He would grab me by my hair and force my face into his crotch, then call me "maricon," (faggot,) and tell me, "You like bicho," (penis) and tell me how disgusting I was. I would just endure this abuse, because I didn't know what to say or do. He was a strong guy, so I quickly started to avoid them both as much as possible, by taking refuge at my relatives' house.

I was so happy when he left! Then shortly after that, I got the news that we were moving to New York. My young life at the age of eight was about to change yet again. Would it finally be for the better this time?

Do not wait: the time will never be 'just right'. Start where you stand, and work whatever tools you may have at your command and better tools will be found as you go along." Napoleon Hill.

CHAPTER 3

Dolores and my father decided to move to New York City, so he sold his bar in Puerto Rico and moved us there. I now assume that it was more her decision than his, because the move meant that she would no longer have to compete with all of the women he met while owning a bar and now she could have him all to herself. As for me, nobody asked or cared what I thought - pretty much par for the course for my life back then.

My first impression of America was not a good one. The neighborhood that we moved to in the Bronx was an absolute hellhole: abandoned, boarded up buildings and the burned out hulks of cars dotted the streets-cape. Raggedy, bearded bums sprawled in doorways, lying in their own filth as they sloshed down brown-bagged bottles of hooch. Graffiti covered every flat surface.

The inhabitants seemed like shell-shocked survivors of a fierce battle zone. Gangs roamed the streets, armed, dangerous and always with a warlike mentality. Their enemy was the cops, and anybody else who got in their way. They ruled the area with an iron fist, controlling everything from prostitution, to drugs to street robbery and all kinds of other scams.

Our apartment was right in the middle of all this madness. When I first saw the six-story building that was to be our "home," it looked like it was abandoned, because it was so filthy and dilapidated. It had huge, wide staircases and a broken-down elevator. In any case, this place was the smallest one-bedroom apartment I had ever seen, and there were six of us, as Estel had come with us as well. The state of disrepair in this tenement was beyond belief. In the bathroom floor, right next to the toilet, there was a huge hole through which you could actually see down into the bathroom downstairs, which my father covered up with a piece of wood.

Dolores became fast friends with the downstairs neighbors, actually having conversations through the hole in the bathroom floor. I even had a few conversations that way myself when they needed to talk to Dolores. I considered the arrangement more weird than convenient.

The apartment was so tiny that we made the living room into a bedroom for us three kids (Dolores' two sons and me) and Estel. We had a small TV in there, and that was the only amenity. Dolores and my dad had the bedroom and a large TV, and they spent most of their time in there. The kitchen was so small that only Estel used it since she was the one who did all the cooking and dishwashing.

It didn't take long for my dad to find a job at a nearby food market. I sometimes wished that I was old enough to have a job too, if only so I didn't have to spend so much time in that rotten little, claustrophobic apartment.

Our building was literally surrounded by garbage! It was an island in a sea of refuse. We used to just open a window, and throw our garbage out from our fifth floor unit; most people in that ghastly neighborhood did the same. There was a vacant lot outside our building, in which grew a huge mountain of garbage. The smell was overwhelming, especially on hot summer days. On such days, you couldn't keep the windows open, or you might actually pass out from the stench.

A lot of people had long clotheslines running from building to building on which they would hang their laundry out to dry. What a sight it was, all these clothes just flapping in the breeze or gracefully rustling right above that giant trash heap. Sometimes, people would light fires in the garbage cans to get rid of at least some of it. The acrid smoke filled the air, and I remember holding my nose so that I wouldn't throw up from the nauseating odor.

It was stifling hot that first summer and we had no air conditioning, just fans blowing around the humid, sticky air in our tiny apartment. The fans, of course, were all but useless, so we suffered dreadfully. Moreover, the apartment was as shabby as it was uncomfortable, tastelessly "decorated" with whatever junk we found on the streets, or that people gave us. Nothing matched with anything else, so it looked like a bad resale show on its worst day. Even at my young age, I could sense that this was a pretty pathetic way to have to live.

They signed me up for school soon after we had moved in. The area's public school was mostly African-American and Puerto Rican. The only whites were students who were basically the poorest children in the city, along with some of the teachers. The area around the school was as much a nightmare as our apartment. Outside the dirty windows of the dingy classrooms, most pedestrians were meandering drug addicts and prostitutes. There were also very colorful cars with big wheel rims, just a few of them brand new. These belonged to the pimps and drug dealers, and stood out starkly from the garbage and the other, old clunker cars. All in all, this hell on Earth made my Aunt Amelia's place in Cantera, with its tropical paradise setting, look like Beverly Hills.

While this place was a huge step down from what I'd known in Puerto Rico, I did eve actually get used to it – sort of.

My biggest problem was that I didn't know a word of English (the first word I learned was the "F word"!). I only spoke Spanish, so I never knew what the hell was going on at school, when I had an assignment or when some of the kids tried to talk to me. It was deeply frustrating, like being in some kind of weird alien world. I'd sit there for hours, reminiscing about my home back in Puerto Rico. I started hanging out with the black kids, even though I didn't understand them, and they didn't understand me. We just started communicating by a primitive form of sign language. I remember them gesturing to me to come with them.

Wanting to fit in and badly needing friends, I'd tag along with them. They would go to the market, to some big store like Woolworth and other stores that carried toys and school supplies. But we weren't there for legitimate shopping. These kids were teaching me how to shoplift, and I quickly discovered that they were quite good at it. I soon became a pro at it just like them, all the time communicating only by sign language. If you remember that all of us were living in some of the most extreme poverty, doing this may seem less immoral. What could be more "wrong" than that little children should have to live in such awful distress and privation? Anyway, I guess it really is true, when they say that necessity is the mother of invention.

My backpack would be crammed full of all the small stuff that I could cram in there from the stores: tiny soldiers, toys, candies, notebooks, pencils, and lots of useless little novelty items. I got so good at "boosting" that wherever I went into one of these places, I could steal stuff on my own, with no need for accomplices. I learned to carry my backpack with me everywhere. It was pretty much the only possession that I had in this world. I would never leave it behind! I even used to sleep with it using it as a pillow.

One day, I went with my dad to the store downstairs from our dumpy apartment, and while he was buying groceries, I was stealing candy. So my dad paid for the groceries and we left the store. Then he noticed me eating the candy I had boosted, and asked me where I got it. I told him, from the store. Then he opened my backpack. Wide eyed he looked over all my loot, and beat the crap out of me, right there in the street with everyone watching. He then took me back to the store, and made me return all of the candy and apologize to the store owner.

Back in the apartment, he took away all my stolen stuff and told Dolores and Estel what I had done, which was profoundly humiliating. He was good at punishment; he spilled rice in a corner of the apartment and made me kneel on it. If you have never knelt on rice before let me tell ya, it's torture like a thousand needles piercing my skin. Dolores delighted in my pain. She scoffed at me to her kids. "Look! Look! Look at him! He's a thief! Stay away from him!"

Her taunting indignation would later drive me almost insane with fury, for reasons you will understand as my story goes on.

After that, once my father went to work and I got back from school, she'd lock me out of the apartment. She made me sit outside until my father came home around seven each night. By this time, it was autumn, and it started to get cold outside, so I was stuck sitting in that dirty stairway, huddled up and freezing! Estel would fight with her to let me in, but Dolores stubbornly refused, saying, "No! No! I don't want my kids around this thief!"

My father kept finding me out there every time he came home, so he would bring me in, and started arguing with her about it too. They were loud, so the whole building could hear them, especially the lady downstairs, through that hole in the bathroom floor. She'd even join in the fray calling out, "You can't do that to him. He's just a kid. He can freeze out there!"

My savior, on this as at many other times, was Estel. If Dolores wasn't home when I returned from school, she would always let me in and would always feed me. Nevertheless, Dolores and I would get into some vicious fights, just as we had done back in Puerto Rico. Most were arguments she contrived as a pretext for mistreating me. She would slap me, hit me with a broomstick, fling heavy glass ashtrays at me, and even throw me against a hot iron! To say that my whole life at this time was "horrendous" would be a gross understatement. As primitive and hard as my existence had sometimes been back in Puerto Rico, going to the Bronx in comparison was like being cast out of the Garden of Eden.

But by this time, I was getting tired of her abuse, and started defending myself. Once, I took a glass plate and cracked it on her head. I would throw whatever garbage I could grab on her food, while her kids would be jumping on me to defend her. Estel would always try to stop Dolores' cruelty to me, because she felt sorry for me; and in stark, magnificent contrast to her selfish, savage daughter, she was a kind and loving person. And Estel, I know you're not reading this now, but thank you wherever you are!

Financially, things got worse for the family before they got better (which, of course, a little kid like me didn't understand), so my father moved us back to Puerto Rico for a little while. While that move had a lot of drawbacks, at least it delivered me from the urban Hell that had been my first taste of America. The "Big Apple" didn't just have a worm in it, from my point of view, but a cobra.

We moved back to the wooden house we had left, while Dolores was living in the big new house that he'd built her. She wouldn't let me in there for anything! I got stuck using the shower outside and the latrine again. But I did have an ally. Estel and I became even closer. She spent as much time as she could in my company. I used to help her with all the household chores, and she would tell me, "Hector, you are a good kid, don't let anyone tell you any different."

By then, the family, my cousins who had been living across the road had moved to New York, and I never did see them again (except Tono, at my father's funeral), so that refuge was no longer available to me.

I had nowhere to go, and I couldn't stay around Dolores. I don't know why my father put up with her; she must have had a spell on him, or she was super good in the bedroom, calling to mind the "succubus," one of the female demons that entice men to their destruction. This was the first time I saw my father stay with any one woman for so long!

After a few months, Dolores decided that she liked living in New York better, so Dad moved us back there. I don't know what the Hell he could have been thinking then, but from my perspective, it was an absolutely awful decision.

We moved into a slightly bigger apartment in the Bronx, just a few blocks away from where we'd lived before. But even though it was not far away, the difference was like night and day. It was a more family-oriented area, and somewhat cleaner.

It was winter when we moved back and I never had seen or experienced snow before, so at first I liked it, as making snow angels and snowmen was a fun new treat that I thought was really cool. I even tried to eat some of the snow. But all of that got old fast. And I was living there with Dolores and her kids again, but this time no Estel. So boy, was I in trouble, with no protector.

There was a bodega a few blocks from our apartment, and Dolores used to make me go there every morning to buy milk, long French bread and a few other items. Instead of money, she gave me a book of food stamps to pay. Actually, I didn't mind running these errands too much, because I would do anything to be away from her. After the store, I went to school, but once again couldn't get used to the environment, and still couldn't communicate, so I started pretending to go to school, but actually would go hang out in our old neighborhood, where I knew the kids.

I would spend the days with the drug addicts, dope dealers and gang bangers. I remember helping some of them to shoot up heroin: They would ask me to tighten some rubber thing around their arms, then they would inject the needle into their bulging veins. Bruises covered every part of their body. I also used to help them hold a spoon while they would cook the heroin, and some of them just passed out right there in front of me after they got high. Most of the time when they needed more "junk," they were already too high to go themselves, so they sent me.

These drug houses were very scary places, but the people there already knew me, so I wasn't too scared. When the addicts didn't have any money to buy their drugs they would break into people's apartments and use me as a lookout. I even knew some of the people whose apartments they broke into, but my first loyalty was to my new friends. They protected me so I would never squeal on them.

One horrifying time, I remember being in a third floor apartment when some guy walked into the living room and started raving like a crazy person. Then, my jaw dropped as he suddenly jumped out the window! And the worst part was that no one else there even cared! Supposedly he had just done some drug called the "pink elephant" which was taken through the eye, like putting in a contact lens. The effects were dangerous, as this incident graphically proved! It made this poor devil feel as big and as tall as an elephant, so when he jumped out the window, he apparently thought he was already close to the sidewalk.

When I heard the wail of a siren in the distance, I knew someone had called the cops. It was like a movie scene, cops and fire trucks everywhere.

My father eventually found out what I was doing, so he came looking for me, and found me at this dark, dirty apartment in the midst of all these derelicts laying around. And yes, once again he beat the crap out of me, saying, "Why aren't you in school?"

After that, I did actually go to school - but school still just wasn't for me! It was like I was in a zone all the time, far away from my loathsome physical surroundings, like I had built a bubble around me, and just couldn't learn anything. The only thing I could get into was Art class. It allowed me to express myself in ways that were simply not available to me at home. My dad punished me by ordering me to come home right after school - into the lioness's den, with Miss Dolores.

There was a thick tension in our house all the time, and I just wanted to be out of there, so badly. I didn't have a bedroom to escape to, since my bedroom was the living room, and Dolores wouldn't let me near her kids, so I couldn't share their bedroom. It would have been an overwhelmingly dispiriting situation for anyone, and I was still a child, just nine.

This brings me back to that incident noted before, when she had told her kids of me, "Look at him. He's a thief!" Well, the appalling irony of it all was that that wicked woman was teaching her own kids how to steal! It's simply disgusting – but not surprising - to realize how much of a hypocrite she truly was.

Our apartment building was owned by an older sophisticated woman who was always well dressed. Dolores became friends with her, so they started doing things together. She would come eat upstairs in our apartment, and we went downstairs to use her phone, since we didn't have one. So Dolores started to basically fake being nice to me and even told her kids, "Don't fight with your big brother." You may be able to imagine how shocked I was by that, but at the same time, I felt relieved. The truth was, since every vestige of love was absent from my life then, I wanted to be loved so badly that when anyone showed me even affection the size of a grain of sand I would get attached immediately. I was that needy.

What was really going on, however, was that Dolores had concocted a supposed "game" that was actually a burglary. In this game, I was the giant man, and her kids (a couple years younger) were the midgets. She had me watch for when our landlady left for work, and one day, as soon as she left, I would tell Dolores, and she'd send me and her two boys into the landlady's closet to steal two of her dresses. I was to take the dresses and hand them to her boys, since I was a "giant," and they couldn't reach the hangers.

The lady used to leave her front door unlocked, so if Dolores needed the phone for anything, she could just go in. The building only had two floors, with a spiral like staircase by the entrance and a long hallway with French doors at the end, which led to the lady's apartment. As an experienced thief even at such a young age, for me, this "game" was just too easy.

Dolores already knew which dresses she wanted, so we got them and I gave them to her kids, who ran upstairs with them. I was still downstairs trying to close the antique armoire that held the dresses so I was last to come up. When I got upstairs, her kids were jumping up and down with glee, twirling around the living room, thrilled that we got the dresses, and me so happy that I was able to please her. Yes, she was a horrible monster to me, but like I said, I was incredibly needy back then, starving for even a semblance of affection and acceptance.

A few days later, the lady came upstairs and told Dolores that a few of her dresses were missing and Dolores, a great actress, said, "Oh my

God! Really? How did it happen?" I think that the lady knew that we took the dresses. I could tell by the angry expression on her face. She didn't accuse us, however, since she had no evidence, but after that, she didn't leave the door open anymore.

This confrontation happened on a weekday. That weekend, Dolores wanted to go dancing, and the stupid cow actually wore one of the stolen dresses. It was green and black, with rhinestones on it. Dolores came out of the bedroom, admittedly looking really beautiful in it. She wore a short rabbit fur coat she got from my father over the dress. She and Dad started walking down the stairs to go out, when the landlady came out and saw her with the dress, and became enraged. She went off on her! Dolores was kind of loud and bellowed, "I don't know what you're talking about! Hector gave me this dress as a gift!" Of course, it was now obvious that her true motive for being nice to me all along was so she could frame me, in case she got caught.

When my father stormed back up the stairs and demanded that I tell him where I got the dress, he was furious! I was already petrified of him, so afraid of getting a truly fierce beating, I told him the truth. Dolores started yelling and saying things like, "I can't believe you, you fucking little thief! Don't try to blame this on me and my kids! We are decent people, and we don't steal. You're the only thief here!"

"Snap," went the camel's back! I blew up like a bombshell, didn't even care that my dad was there. I threw myself on Dolores and started biting her, pulling her hair, and spitting. I ripped the dress off her, and started breaking things. I was using strength that I didn't know I had. Not even my father could stop me! I was beet red, shaky, and absolutely berserk!

Since I already had the reputation of being a thief, she figured my father would believe her. But the kind of behavior I displayed at that moment was similar to how he'd seen me act after his brother raped me, when he was going to take me back there. So finally he figured it all out. It took him forever, but at last it dawned on him that this woman was a lying, sadistic bitch who hated me. When I realized that he had grasped the situation, a spark of hope lit up in me, as I thought that I would be going home to Puerto Rico after that.

Yeah right! I should be so lucky! Unfortunately for me, it turned out that the reason they were going out was to celebrate her pregnancy; she was going to surprise my father with the news. Well, it sure surprised me! And it meant that now my dad had a new reason not to dump her. Several months later, my half-sister Cindy was born in New York.

I am a bit nervous about Cindy's reaction if and when she reads all this, because as far as I know, she knew nothing about her mom's dishonesty, or how criminally she had treated me. But I have long since just moved on with my life, and am at peace with myself. So, sister, if you're reading this book, I am sorry for the abominable truths about your mother that you will learn from it.

Cindy and I were not raised together, and we don't have any bad feelings towards each other. We talk once in a blue moon, and when we do, we can chat for hours. She has three beautiful kids and a husband who adores her. They have been together for many years, and I hope they will continue to be happy. She deserves it: After all, everyone needs to be loved.

By the way, we were also born on the same day, Oct 2nd, as was our father. Sometimes it's almost impossible for me to believe that circumstances like this could be mere coincidence. Strange and mysterious things just seem to be a part of life – and maybe that's the way it's supposed to be.

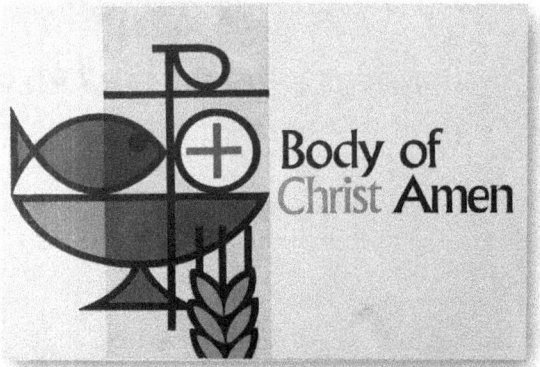

La Communion

Aim to be the most wonderful and outstanding self that you can be and unremittingly continue your ascent! Faith means having the heart of challenge to be fearless, and to take action toward your personal growth and development. **Daisaku Ikada.**

CHAPTER 4

❧

My father decided to move me to Chicago in 1971, when I was about ten or eleven, more than likely because Dolores wanted me gone. All I remember is the two of us getting on a plane in New York. I thought I was finally going home to Puerto Rico. Though at the time I hadn't realized just how homesick I was, that was indeed where I considered home to be. However, my father hadn't told me where he was taking me...and I soon found out that I was wrong about returning to Puerto Rico.

When we arrived in Chicago, he brought me to his sister, my Aunt Nivia's apartment. I had met her when I was younger, but had totally forgotten about her. The only person I remembered in that apartment was my cousin Sonia, because we'd accidentally burned down a closet together while playing at my house in Puerto Rico.

There were lots of new faces there, five cousins (three boys, two girls, including Sonia), and my aunt. She was divorced and there was no man in the house. My other aunt, Rosa, lived upstairs with her five kids (also three boys and two girls). I didn't know them, and had no idea who they were. My father dropped me off with Nivia and returned to New York the next day.

I still didn't speak any English and was confused about everything. What was supposed to happen next? Where do I go? Do I sit? Do I stand? I was just there, surrounded by strangers, and not knowing anything. Even though I was petrified of my dad, I somehow felt like

I belonged with him, so when he left the next day, I sort of felt numb, telling myself, "Oh well, he'll be back." Furthermore, since I really had no great affection for my father, I didn't much care that he had gone, other than that I was now alone in a completely unfamiliar setting. Nonetheless, I felt hurt.

Aunt Rosa was more easygoing with her kids, whereas Aunt Nivia was super strict with hers. And just my luck, it was Nivia who my father had left me with.

Immediately, my aunt started giving me chores and tried treating me like one of her own. They lived across the street from the Wicker Park Grammar School, which had a huge playground you could see from her living room window. At the beginning, I used to just look out the windows or sit on the stairs and watch the girls play jump rope and the guys play softball.

But little by little, though I felt empty and hurt, I started to find my way into this new life. I wanted to go home to Puerto Rico. I didn't want to be where I was, but had no choice.

My aunt started to notice how resistant and disrespectful I was to her (and for that matter, to everyone else). One day, she was ironing and told me to do something. I just looked at her and told her in a nasty way, "Fuck you!" (At the time, all I knew in English were a few curse words). Well, she had this TV cord tied up like a very thin snake that she used to hit her kids when they misbehaved. She started hitting me with it around my feet; the sting was like having a thousand piranhas biting at the same time!

By this point in my life, I was already confused about what was appropriate behavior, and disturbed by many of my experiences in the world, so I defended myself like a wild animal would do. I didn't know the difference between discipline and sheer cruelty, so I took the hot iron and threw it at her, and started kicking things around the room.

She had a shocked look on her face when I actually fought back, and of course this led to being punished. My cousins in the dining room were just watching all of this, probably wondering what the hell was wrong with me. They loved their mother, but were also completely terrified of her. They would never talk back to her, or even think of raising a hand to her. I must admit that even though she was fearsomely strict, her children have turned out to be quite decent people to this very day.

Now, as an adult, I realize that she had to be that strict, because we lived in a neighborhood that was not very safe. In fact, it was downright dangerous. There were gang bangers everywhere and all sorts of hazardous things happening, like gang fights, shootings, and drug activity. She had a curfew and her kids had to be home by 8 p.m. Fortunately, since the Wicker Park Grammar School (which we attended, and we played there too) was right across the street, she could always keep an eye out to make sure we were all right. She told us to always stay where she could see us, and if we were to go somewhere else, we had to tell her first.

Hector M. Abreu

EXPLICACION DE NOTAS

APROVECHAMIENTO

La letra indica la calidad del trabajo de su hijo:

E — Excelente
G — Bueno
F — Promedio
U — Deficiente

ESFUERZO

El número indica cuanto su hijo se esfuerza:

1 — Hace lo mejor posible
2 — Podría hacer más
3 — Hace muy poco

La señal (√) indica que su hijo necesita mejorar en este aspecto

NIVELES DE TRABAJO

AL — A nivel avanzado
GL — A nivel normal
BL — A nivel bajo

NOTAS CUMULATIVAS

3.1

	10° Semana	20° Semana	30° Semana	40° Semana
1.9 Nivel de trabajo	BL	BL	BL	BL
LECTURA	G 2	G 2	b 2	b 2
Conoce palabras				
Comprende lo que lee	√	√		
Interpreta lo que lee	√	√		
Localiza y usa información	√	√		
Aprecia buena literatura				
Nivel de trabajo	B L	BL	BL	BL
MATEMATICAS	F 2	G 2	b 2	b 2
Comprende conceptos	√			
Puede usar números				
Puede resolver problemas	√	√		

CAPACIDADES, INTERESES Y SERVICIOS ESPECIALES

_____

_____

Nombre del alumno __Hector Abreu__

	10° Semana	20° Semana	30° Semana	40° Semana
ESCUCHAR	b 2	G 2	7 2	b 2
Comprende lo que oye Interpreta lo que oye	√			
HABLAR	7 2	F 2	7 2	b 2
Puede comunicar ideas				
Habla claramente y distintamente	√	√		
ESCRIBIR	7 2	G 2	7 2	b 2
Escribe efectivamente	√	√		
Escribe obras creativas	√	√		
Usa destrezas fundamentales correctamente	√	√		
Caligrafía — Escribe con legibilidad				
ORTOGRAFIA	b 2	G 2	b 2	b 2
Aprende las palabras designadas				
Deletrea correctamente	√	√		
CIENCIA	b 2	F 2	b 2	b 2
Comprende conceptos fundamentales				
Puede resolver problemas	√	√		
ESTUDIOS SOCIALES	7 3	F+ 2	7 3	7 2
Comprende conceptos fundamentales	√	√		
Desarrolla las destrezas para comprender los mapas y el globo	√	√		
ARTE	b	G	b	E
EDUCACION MUSICAL	b	G	b	b
EDUCACION FISICA	E 1	E 2	E 2	E 2
	b 1	G 2	7	b

RASGOS DE CONDUCTA

El alumno tiene que demostrar progreso en los hábitos sociales, de trabajo y de salud para realizar las ventajas máximas del programa educacional. La señal (✔) indica que su hijo necesita mejorar. Si no hay señal indica progreso satisfactorio.

	10° Semana	20° Semana	30° Semana	40° Semana
RASGOS SOCIALES				
Puede contenerse	✓	✓		
Escucha con cortesía				
Obedece las reglas de la escuela				
Acepta responsabilidad por lo que hace				
Respeta los derechos de otros				
Respeta la propiedad ajena				
HABITOS DE TRABAJO				
Tiene y cuida su material, y está preparado a trabajar				
Obedece direcciones				
Hace trabajo ordenado			✓	
Puede trabajar por sí mismo	✓	✓		
Puede pensar por sí mismo				
Entrega su trabajo a tiempo				
HABITOS DE SALUD Y DE SEGURIDAD				
Obedece las reglas de salud				
Está limpio				
Se viste en ropa propia				
Obedece las reglas de seguridad				

FIRMA DEL PADRE O ENCARGADO

Ramona Cruz _____ (10° semana)
Ramona Cruz _____ (20° semana)
Ramona Cruz _____ (30° semana)

ULTIMO INFORME

PROMOVIDO _X_   RETENIDO _____

GRADO EL PROXIMO AÑO __6__   SALON __306__

(81. 132—Span.)

ESCUELAS PUBLICAS DE CHICAGO

JAMES F. REDMOND
Superintendente General de Escuelas

GRADOS 4-6

INFORME DE PROGRESO ESCOLAR

19_73_ a 19_74_

Nombre del alumno _Hector Abreu_

_17231308_
Número del alumno

Escuela _WICKER PARK_

Dirección de la escuela   2009 W. SCHILLER ST.

Salón _309_   Grado _5_

Maestro _Mrs. Mayer_

Principal _Emilie A. Lepthorn_

PUNTUALIDAD

Es muy importante que su hijo asista a la escuela con regularidad y que llegue a tiempo. Cuando falte a clases o llegue tarde se requiere una carta del padre o encargado explicando la ausencia o la tardanza.

	10° SEMANA	20° SEMANA	30° SEMANA	40° SEMANA
DIAS DE AUSENCIA	1	0	7	0
TARDANZAS	0	1	0	0

Muy señores míos:

El maestro de su hijo, el principal y todos nosotros verdaderamente nos interesamos en el desarrollo y el progreso de su hijo. Este informe, despachado cuatro veces durante el año escolar, es uno de los medios empleados por la escuela para informarles del crecimiento educacional de su hijo.

Que Vds. tomen parte en el progreso de su hijo es muy importante. Le ayudará mucho a su hijo si Vds. cada vez que reciban este informe, estudien cada artículo con el niño.

Si tienen preguntas con respecto a este informe o el progreso de su hijo, esperamos que Vds. visiten la escuela. Queremos que Vds. confieran con el maestro quien está deseoso de tomar parte con Vds. en el desarrollo de su hijo.

S. S. S.

James F. Redmond
Superintendente General de Escuelas

Please stay in school and finish your education

CHICAGO PUBLIC SCHOOLS

OUTDOOR EDUCATION AND CAMPING PROGRAM

This

Certificate

Is Awarded to

Hecter Abreu

Cabin 18

in recognition of

achievement as a

Camper

WILLIAM BEVERLY

Camp Coordinator

Title 1, E.S.E.A.

CHICAGO PUBLIC SCHOOLS

OUTDOOR EDUCATION AND CAMPING PROGRAM

This

Certificate

Is Awarded to

HECTOR ABREU

CABIN 18

in recognition of
achievement in

Honor Cabin

wednesday

WILLIAM BEVERLY

Camp Coordinator

Title 1, E.S.E.A.

CHICAGO PUBLIC SCHOOLS

OUTDOOR EDUCATION AND CAMPING PROGRAM

This **Certificate**

Is Awarded to

Hector Abreu

Cabin 18

in recognition of

achievement in a

Special Project

3rd PLACE HONOR CABIN

WILLIAM BEVERLY

Camp Coordinator

Title 1, E.S.E.A.

After a few rough "settling in" incidents like that, it wasn't long before I pretty much forgot about my father, and started getting used to my new environment. It felt homey, safe, motherly like. There were lots of cousins to be with, argue with, make up with, watch cartoons ("Tom and Jerry," "Popeye," "Speed Racer," etc.) every Saturday and Sunday morning with. I also got to experience "normal" things that most people take for granted, like a Christmas party, Christmas trees and gifts, New Year's, birthdays and summer barbecues (I especially remember salami and cheese and French bread sandwiches) to enjoy as a family. I started to feel "loved" somehow, even though I felt like it was likely to be taken away from me soon. I just kept waiting to be moved again.

For the first time, I was actually surrounded by a normal family, unlike the poverty, cruelty and chaos of my life before. Living with my Aunt Nivia was my first experience of many ordinary childhood activities like getting up in the morning, having breakfast, being given lunch money, and coming back home right after school. After getting home, we all sat around the dining room table to do our homework until it was done, then we would have dinner, do some household chores and watch a little TV. Then we would go outside for a while before bed by 8 or 9 p.m. For the first time, I began to realize that life didn't have to be as horrible as it had been with my father and Dolores: It didn't have to be a fight for survival, with pain or poverty always lurking in the shadows.

Before bed, my aunt would have us each take a bath, so in the mornings all we had to do was get dressed and brush our teeth before school.

My Aunt Nivia received public assistance. Since she now had a new mouth to feed, she had me added to her food stamp allotment and got me a medical card. Then she started to notice that I couldn't hear well, and that there was often moist pus on my pillowcases. Also around that time, she found me in a corner of the family room in the middle of the night, huddling in the dark. I was crying very quietly because I was afraid to get in trouble, but she could still hear me. I was in pain because I had yet another agonizing ear infection, which I'd been getting since the car accident at age five. As time passed, that problem just got worse. That night was when it really intensified, and felt like the whole right side of my head was burning, dripping, pus oozing out of my ear; the pain became overwhelming.

She turned on a lamp next to the sofa, near where I was hiding when she found me. I was afraid that it would seem like I was causing trouble, and thought she was going to give me a beating, but she seemed sincerely concerned about my distress, very kindly asking me what was wrong with me, and gently pulling me out of the corner. I told her, in a very scared voice, that my ear was hurting terribly. She started asking me where, and which ear, and I showed her my whole side was red and hot, and she saw the pus coming out of my ear. She still spoke to me in this motherly voice, though shocked now. She asked me, "Does your father know about this?"

I told her yes.

"Has he taken you to a doctor?" she asked.

I said, "No," so she actually just hugged me and stayed up with me, trying to comfort me! I had never had anyone do that for me before, and it felt so good that even though I was in pain, I felt as though I had an actual mother for the first time in my life, and just started crying like I never had before. I just let all my dammed-up feelings out. When my aunt saw this, she knew that there was more to anguish like mine than just my ear pain. I never forgot the experience of seeing her horror at realizing what I must have been through in my life.

I even thanked her for it as an adult, in 2008. Moreover, as I am writing about this, I have tears streaming from my eyes, thinking about that awful, but wonderful, long ago night.

The very next morning, she took me to an ear specialist. They did all sorts of exams, and gave me ear-drops, but the pain got worse before it got better. They tried many things, but eventually they had to give me ear surgery. The first operation didn't work and neither did the second one. Finally, the third operation =– which I didn't have until I was 21 years old – cured me, delivering me from recurrent pain that had seemed likely to last all my life. But by the time I got real medical attention, my eardrum was rotten, and had to be removed. If my father had taken proper care of me when I got hit by the car, they would have had been able to save my eardrum. But then, this kind of failure was all too typical of how he treated me: Almost like I was just an inconvenience and an afterthought.

I remember so many trips with my aunt back and forth to the doctors, and how she was distraught that they couldn't cure my ear. I used to look at her while she talked to the doctors, saying things like, "Hay! Dios mio, pobresito, hay que a ber algo para cularlo," which means, "My God, there has to be something to cure him, he's really suffering!" She would go to the hospital with me each time I had surgery, which was time clawed out of her busy life to take care of me. Witnessing her concern and affection, I started to see a different side of the world. When all this happened, it was new and amazing for me to actually have somebody care for me so much and in this way. And every time I saw her, my face lit up like a Christmas tree. I started to do everything she would tell me to do, just like her kids did.

Around the time she discovered my ear injury, my aunt also started getting calls from my school, because the teachers noticed that I never seemed to pay attention, and was always off in some world of my own. Of course, the reason for that was that I still didn't really understand English. The teachers wanted to know what was wrong with this kid, he's not learning anything and does not cooperate well with other children.

Well, my aunt came up with a solution to that. She had her kids (who were bilingual) speak only English in my presence. There was no Spanish allowed around me, and when she caught them trying to help me out, she would make them put a quarter in a jar. Well yes, the jar did get somewhat full, but my cousins' efforts for me increasingly made me feel like part of the family. She also had them help me with my homework, and sent me to summer school. Summer school! I didn't even know that existed! I believe to this day that she and my Aunt Rosa told their kids to look after me and help me out whenever and wherever they could.

It's like they'd finally realized that I was a wild little animal who was kind (and wounded), but who needed training, so that is what they did. Between both of my aunts and my ten cousins (their children), I started to see a new world full of possibilities. I lived with my aunt for about three years.

I remember when (long before my "domestication" by my aunt started to take hold) I got my first report card from Wicker Park Grade School. Initially, my grades were very bad, but eventually they climbed from F's to levels like BL, which means normal. F2 meant a bit better than F, he can do much more; and E was for excellent… the grade I got in Art of course. I was thrilled about it, even though my other grades were still bad and Aunt Nivia told me, "This is good, Hector, so I am going to send you to summer camp. But you have to promise you will do better in school." I still have the report card with the precious "E."

In those three years, I had some wonderful teachers. They were kind, soft-spoken, patient, and they were a lot like therapists at the same time. To this day, I am still thankful to them and to my Chicago cousins for all the motivation they helped me develop.

I started to get school merit certificates for achieving certain tasks and small projects, and even joined a school play called "Latin American Day." I got certificates for a special project, one in physical education, a camper certificate of merit, one for service room helper, one for summer camp and the Latin American play. Such things might seem like quaint, unimportant childhood rites to many people, but to me, coming from the savage, primitive life I'd known up to now, they were indescribably precious, proof of my progress from being little more than a speaking animal to being an actual, functioning Person. I

My first and only school program

still have all those certificates and the play program. I even have two classroom pictures.

Considering the savage, primitive life I had, these certificates were like solid gold bars to me. They were proof of my progress. They indicated I was skilled, talented and capable. They offered a glimmer of hope that maybe, just maybe, I was someone special.

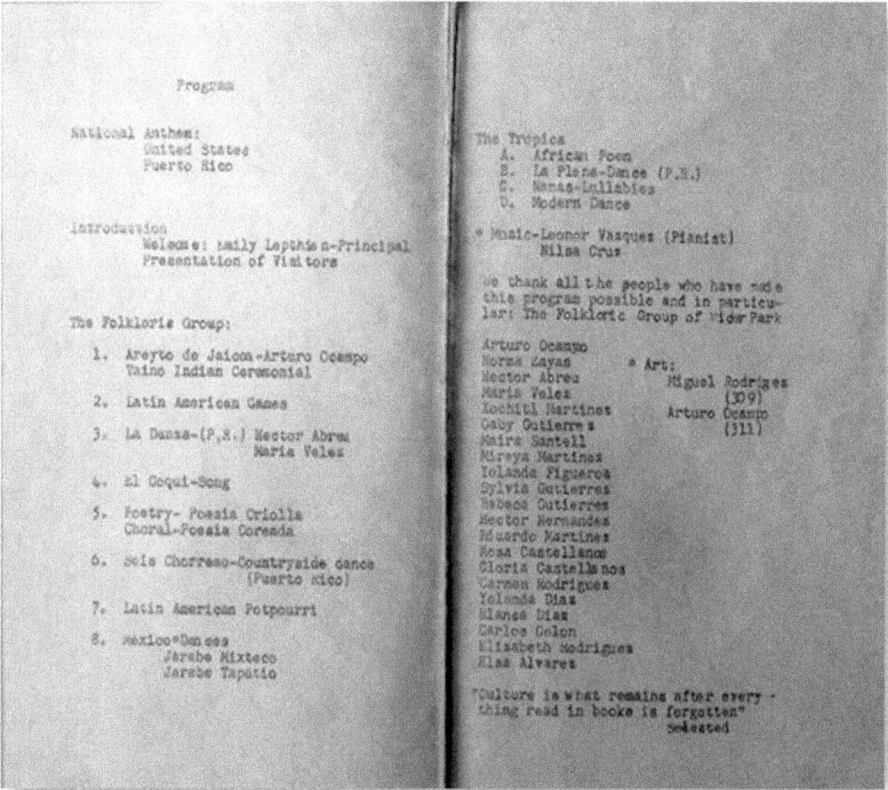

Program

National Anthem:
    United States
    Puerto Rico

Introduction
    Welcome: Emily Lapthisen-Principal
    Presentation of Visitors

The Folkloric Group:

1. Areyto de Jaicoa-Arturo Ocampo
   Taino Indian Ceremonial

2. Latin American Games

3. La Danza-(P.R.) Hector Abreu
   Maria Velez

4. El Coqui-Song

5. Poetry- Poesia Criolla
   Choral-Poesia Coreada

6. Seis Chorreao-Countryside dance
   (Puerto Rico)

7. Latin American Potpourri

8. Mexico-Dances
   Jarabe Mixteco
   Jarabe Tapatio

The Tropics
  A. African Poem
  B. La Plena-Dance (P.R.)
  C. Nanas-Lullabies
  D. Modern Dance

* Music-Leonor Vasquez (Pianist)
   Nilsa Cruz

We thank all the people who have made this program possible and in particular: The Folkloric Group of Wilder Park

Arturo Ocampo
Norma Zayas
Hector Abreu
Maria Velez
Xochitl Martinez
Gaby Gutierrez
Maira Santell
Mireya Martinez
Iolanda Figueroa
Sylvia Gutierrez
Rebeca Gutierrez
Hector Hernandez
Eduardo Martinez
Rosa Castellanos
Gloria Castellanos
Carmen Rodriguez
Yolanda Diaz
Blanca Diaz
Carlos Colon
Elizabeth Rodriguez
Elsa Alvaret

* Art:
  Miguel Rodriguez
  (309)
  Arturo Ocampo
  (311)

"Culture is what remains after everything read in books is forgotten"
    Selected

Times of difficult struggles are opportunities to accomplish our human revolution. **Daisaku Ikada**

CHAPTER 5

❧

IN 1974, WHEN I WAS almost 13 and had been living in Chicago with my Aunt Nivia for three years, I got the news that my father was moving to Chicago, with Dolores, whom I now began calling, at least in my mind, the Cookie Monster. (Her nickname was actually "Cookie," which was what the family called her). When he arrived, I just looked at him. He tapped me on the head and told me, "We are moving with your sister, Maggie. You have a little sister now." Maggie was Cindy's birth name.

Scared as I was of him, I became defiant. I told him I wanted to stay with Aunt Nivia. My aunt didn't say anything but it felt like she didn't want me to go. She had gotten attached to me, and I had become very comfortable with her whole family. I was doing great there, and had more or less forgotten I even had a father. After all, we hadn't bonded in any way, and I really didn't even like him.

Of course, my father paid no attention to my protests. He found an apartment and moved Dolores and her three kids to Chicago. He also pulled me out of school and signed me up to a school near the new place. He arranged our lives just like he had in New York. He got a job at some factory or restaurant - I can't remember. All I knew was that he wasn't around much from morning to late evenings.

So once again I found myself alone with Dolores a lot. She started having me take care of my sister and her other two kids, and do all the house chores, making excuses to the authorities for my absence from school while her own kids went and got educated. She would disappear for hours just about every day. This was because while she was in New York, she had met a man named Luis and she was cheating on my father with him.

Then Luis moved to Chicago to be near her. After about a month or so, she moved in with Luis and told me, "Don't worry, your father will come for us. Later, we are moving to a new place."

We moved in, and here was this strange, new handsome face, who was actually very nice to her and all the kids, including me. Dolores just had me babysit and clean. While she was on her new honeymoon, I was being "Cinderella," doing all the dirty work.

I didn't really know she was cheating on my dad. She and Luis never did anything romantic in front of me, so I didn't know what was really going on. All I do remember was that about two weeks later, my father showed up at the door and told me to get my stuff. I thought he was coming to stay and since he was always disappearing I didn't think much of that. But then he glared at Cookie and told her, *"Tu eres una puta Sucia!"* which means, "You're a dirty whore!"

He moved me to a different apartment on a street that happened to be called Wicker Park, which was also the name of neighborhood and the grammar school I had attended. He signed me up in a different school, Anderson High School, which I believe is still there, on Division Street, near Damen Avenue. It was a small school, in a horrible neighborhood - just like our new apartment. The building had four units, two in front and two in back. The area was filthy and seemed to always be buried in trash. By the way, this area happens to be beautiful now - and expensive.

But that is now. Back then, I walked in and saw a very badly decorated apartment. My father showed me to my bedroom, which was a tiny little box; the stairs from the apartment above took up almost half its space. The unit's front window was so dirty you couldn't see outside; obviously, it hadn't been cleaned for years. In fact, all the windows were like this, which should give some idea of how well maintained this place was. After this cursory showing of my new home, Dad went into his bedroom and fell asleep.

As I was sitting in this strange place with no one to talk to, I felt disoriented, cut off from the familiar, stable life at Aunt Nivia's. So I went outside and sat for several hours on the front stairs of the building, just looking at all the surrounding garbage and kids playing in the filthy front yards nearby. Eventually, my father got up and went to work. He had found a nighttime job, and – typical for his sense of parental responsibility – just left me alone with no explanation or preparations. He told me there was no food there and if I needed anything to call Aunt Nivia, who lived about fifteen minutes away.

By this time, it was summer, so I didn't have school. Dad had signed me up just before the end of the school year. As time passed, I started entertaining myself with cleaning and decorating the squalid little apartment, doing grocery shopping, our laundry, etc. I got very good at decorating at that time. I was still only 12 years old, going on 13. When people, including my Aunt Nivia and cousins came over to visit once in a while (I guess she was checking up on me), they would say, "Wow! This place is so beautiful, it looks like a woman lives here. It's so clean and neat, and so nicely decorated. Everything matches with everything else."

I became friends with the lady upstairs, Esterlina, and her husband Bruno. She was from Colombia and she was very good to me. She would frequently check up on me and made sure I had eaten something. Bruno just always looked at me with this strange, yet familiar look that conveyed, "*hmmm this kid is a fag!*" I heard him a few times tell her and she would always tell him, "Don't bother Hector, leave him alone." They both knew that I was gay. Of course, in my youthful naiveté, I still didn't even know what that meant.

Esterlina started to take me with her everywhere, except her apartment. Bruno didn't really want me there, so when he came home, I would run downstairs. But as I hung out with her, I learned how to get around the new neighborhood, and met all the local ladies. I became friends with all these women, and would spend hours with them. I helped them with their kids, with their house chores, and ran errands for them.

Once these ladies saw what I had done to my own apartment and how I turned it from a dump into a beautiful place, they started having me around to help them with many "refined" activities. Esterlina used to sell Avon, knickknacks, clothing, jewelry, and Stanley household products. She would even make things -- place mats, blouses, flower arrangements, all sorts of things -- to sell, and was teaching me all about these activities. Before I knew it, I was selling anything I could. I even used to host Tupperware parties.

I also used to take my father's food stamps and do a lot of grocery shopping, then would cook as if for ten people, making meals I planned to sell. Then I would go from store to store and sell my pre-made lunches there, and whatever other products I was selling at the time. This would usually be items like rice and beans, steak and onions, franks and bean, chicken stew, etc. Just imagine a twelve year old having Tupperware parties, with an apartment full of women! Too funny – but at least I was making a few dollars. Also, this was when I started to learn how to dress myself and buy the latest fashions and things for the apartment.

To this day, I am still like that; I always want to look fashionable, and love to redo my apartment constantly. Needless to say, I need to move at least every five years or so. I can't stand living in a place too long, or to keep looking at the same décor. I now realize where this tendency comes from: I had been moved so many times as a kid that it has become like a second nature to me. I just wake up in the morning and say, "It's time to move!" I just give most of my stuff away and start a whole new environment. I've done it so much that to me, giving my material stuff away means nothing. I actually have learned to love doing that, giving my things to people who I know, who don't have much. It makes me feel good to see a smile on their faces. Their happiness bounces back on me, sort of like an "offset" to all the trouble and pain I'd known in my own childhood. That's turned out to be part of my "philosophy" which I developed without even really thinking about it. I can be sad and bitter for my past experiences, or I can rejoice in my life and all the good things in it. I reject bitterness, and choose joy. Quite simple, really.

But for now, back to the story of my life on Wicker Park Street. By that first fall living there, I knew most of the ladies in the 'hood. Across the street from where I lived, there was a big apartment building with six units. I became friends with most of the ladies who lived there, especially Lourdes and her husband and two kids. I used to spend most of my evenings at her place. Right after school, I would just go home, drop off my books and go to her house. She loved having me there, because I would help her with everything, including taking care of her kids.

One day, Lourdes went to take a shower, while Eduardo ("Ed," her husband) and I stayed in the living room area, watching the kids. Before I go on, I have to say Eduardo was one hot man! Sort of like the Marlboro cigarette commercial man back in the '70s. He must have known that I was gay, so he asked me to go get something for him. What he asked me to get for him was too high for me (a 13-year old) to reach, up in one of those china cabinet built-ins that came in the apartments. This one was in a tiny hallway that led to the kitchen and the bathroom was across from it.

I told Ed I couldn't reach it. He came over to help, but then stood behind me and started pressing his cock over my butt while we were still dressed. I could feel his small penis; he was not big at all, and he asked me, "You want it?"

I really didn't say much. I basically just grabbed at his member through his pants, then he pulled it out and had me suck him off till he had an orgasm. Then he whispered some very obscene words in my ear.

All of this happened while Lourdes was in the shower, and their kids (just two and three years old) were only a few feet away. Ed figured we wouldn't get caught, since he knew his wife was in the shower, which he could hear running. When Lourdes came out, I had already serviced her husband, and we both acted innocent. She had no idea anything had even happened. Because there was no one at my home and I lived across the street, I used to stay at her place till real late at night. You could see my father's apartment from her living room and hers from mine. At the entrance to her place there was a long hallway, twelve to fifteen feet long, with a door and a closet that led to the dining room. When it was time for me to go home, she would go to bed and have Ed walk me to the door to close it, so he would close the dining room door behind him and walk me to the front door. As we walked he would put his hands down my pants and play with my butt. Then, when we got to the door he would press his cock against my butt and tell me about all of the crude things that he wanted to do to me.

This went on for several months. He loved to walk me to the door and did so almost every night, along with feeling me up. We never did get caught. During my evenings at his place, he used to sit on the front stairs and talk to me with his eyes. He also had some secret hand gestures that no one else would notice and gave me a sign to, "Pull your pants down and show me your butt." He would put a finger in his mouth, to convey that he wanted me to blow him. A few times when Lourdes was asleep, and since he knew I was home alone, he started coming over to my apartment. This was when he started penetrating me.

This is also when I first talked to a man while he was having sex with me. He did me so many times, and in so many positions, that I started to get turned on and not scared anymore. The idea that sex might actually be pleasurable was entirely new to me. Of course, by now, I was no longer a small child, and was approaching puberty.

One day, while Lourdes was in the hospital having their third child, Eduardo had me spend the night with him, in their bed! While their kids were just a few feet away sleeping, he was having sex like there was no one there to hear him. In the morning, his kids woke up and came into their parents' room, while there I was, in bed with their father (the children were toddlers, too young to realize there was anything odd about what they were seeing – or to communicate it to their mother). He treated it like nothing and I didn't think of anything of it either. Why would I? After all, I already thought this sort of encounter was normal; it had long been my "normal."

More important, this was the first time I thought I was in love with a man. Eduardo treated me like his girlfriend. He bought me stuff like candy and was always paying for things while I was out with him and Lourdes and their kids. I say that I was in love because, even though he was actually abusing me (still a minor), I didn't know the difference. He treated me so well, and I would just fall in love with anyone who treated me decently (as I had with my Aunt Nivia, but of course, there was no sexual aspect to my affection for her). I believe he told his brother in law, Manuel, Lourdes' brother, that we were having sex, or at least that I was gay. When I first met Manuel, he had come over to watch the kids while Ed went to the hospital when Lourdes had given birth to their third child. I was shocked at how beautiful he was.

That day, when I came over to Lourdes' place Manuel told me what was going on. The kids were having their daytime nap and Manuel just came out and plainly asked me if I wanted to play with him. He pulled out his member, grabbed me by the head, and made me go down on him. Then he took me to the kitchen and penetrated me while I was standing up. He told me to wash the dishes while he mounted me. After he had his orgasm, he told me to finish doing the dishes.

The reason I believe Ed told him about me was because Manuel just came out and bluntly asked me for sex. Of course I figured this out later on as an adult. Throughout my life I have kept having occasional flashbacks of many of the men who molested me when I was young.

By the time Ed seduced me, I had become really good at having sex with men. It was like I just got addicted to the activity. Soon, I started actually seeking sex, rather than just having it forced on me. This included both teenagers and grown men. For example, I was intimate with the son of a lady who lived a few buildings away, and also with the son of a lady right next door. One day, that neighbor must have been exceptionally excited, because he just took me to a dark hallway and penetrated me while we were still dressed and even wearing our coats. Soon, I also had sex with his brother in law. I just came out and asked him if he wanted to have sex with me. It was late, and there was no one around. He must have been horny as hell, because he jumped on me right away, took me to the back of the building next to where I lived, had me bend over behind a bush, and penetrated me. He liked it so much that one day later, when he found me alone, he asked me if I wanted some more, so we did it in a secluded pathway.

It was around this time when I noticed that, not only could sex be enjoyable, but that I had some type of control over the situation – both of which were new to me. I learned how to boldly ask men if they wanted to penetrate me, and if they wanted me to service them. I became really proficient at sex, and it was the only thing I was never afraid of doing, even though I was still very shy and always on my guard. This realization gave me power, and I felt loved even if it was just for five minutes. I confused real love with mere lust somehow and every time I asked for sex, I got it. Very few guys said no to me. With most guys I desired, I bluntly asked if they were married, single, straight, and even gay - although I still didn't know what a "gay" person was. I thought I was the only one in the world like me, so I always made sure I kept it a secret.

Knowing I had this newfound control, ironically caused me to start getting out of control. As often happens with young people, I got intoxicated with this new experience, and didn't recognize the need for moderation. It seemed like I was having sex with just about every age-appropriate male on our small street. My partners were the boys from across the street, their best friend, and their friend's friends and their fathers, their sons as well as numerous married ladies' husbands and their kids. My routine was to just come up to a stranger and boldly solicit them and usually, they would! I had sex with a few of the gang bangers of the district. I even had regular lovers who came over to my father's place at night while he was working, when I knew he wouldn't be home till morning. I wasn't at all afraid to bring them over.

Only 12 years old, I'd had sex with at least 30 males (voluntarily; not including the ones who had abused me as a child). I had more sex with older men than young kids. Older guys seemed to respond more enthusiastically when I would make overtures to them. Already used to it, I had been doing this sort of thing with grown men since I was seven.

But by the time I entered high school, it was like a whole different ballgame. On my way to my new school, Anderson High, I had to pass the apartment of one of my lady friends. Her husband was out of work, extremely handsome, and I knew he was always home alone in the mornings. So one day, I knocked on their door and he answered it. He told me that his wife had already left, so I brazenly asked if he wanted to have sex with me. I somehow knew that was on his mind. He looked a little surprised, but then checked to make sure no one was looking, and let me into the apartment.

Right away I began to get things started, but he said, "Wait, let's go to the living room." He put a straight porn movie on the television. By this time, he already had an erection visible through his pajamas, so I quickly just started sucking him while he watched the movie. Then we had sex and he kept asking me if I wanted what was happening in the movie. When it was time for him to have his orgasm, I told him, "Give it to me, don't take it out!" It made me feel loved, like I carried proof of someone's love inside me. It made me feel special. So he and I would have sex just about every morning on my way to school.

While I was in my new school, I couldn't care less about learning anything. It was like everything I learned at school while living with my Aunt Nivia went right out the door. All I cared about was staring at guys' crotches, including the male teachers. I started taking workshop classes, and besides the gym showers, this was my favorite place to go to in the school. I looked forward to that class every Friday.

While in workshop they assigned me to work in the camera room (also called the dark room), since I wasn't good at anything else there; all I had to do was turn a light switch on and off. There were three guys assigned to this room. A hot guy named Wilfred, a cute white boy, and another named Bill, a hot Puerto Rican. On the first day we did shop, Wilfred decided to go outside the tiny dark room with me "to help me switch the light." He insisted on it, since he had already seen me scope him out, looking at his crotch.

Because he could tell I lusted for him, he stood behind me - very close since it was a tiny room, perhaps two feet by three, and was covered with a long, heavy black drape. He got very close to me, put his hand on mine to turn the light off, and I started feeling his cock as he pressed it against me. Wasting no time, I reached behind me, and started grabbing for his penis. He was so stiff it felt like he was going to explode right in his pants. He asked me to get on my knees and suck him, which I did, then quickly asked him to have sex with me, which he did.

We got together often and I felt so special every time. We would do it standing up and he would whisper things in my ear like, "You like it, I like it, it feels like when I fuck my girlfriend." We had sex in that tiny little room so many times that I couldn't wait for workshop. I felt so loved because of this routine and every time I saw him in the hallways or classrooms, my heart would start beating faster. When he looked at me, I would just melt. I often used to see him with his girlfriends in the halls, but in my mind, he was thinking of me too, rather than just the babe he was with. I would tell myself, I have his love in me.

After school I would take a different route home and would ask a stranger if he wanted to sex with me. I remember this one guy who happened to live at the end of the block from my father's apartment. Almost every day I came over and simply got on my knees to service him. As a freshman in high school I usually was sexually active with three or four guys a day. When I wasn't, I felt left out, like I was worthless and no one loved me.

When I started getting older and would think about those days, I would ask myself *why am I like this? Why do I do this stuff and why do I love it and feel so wanted when I do?* My guess? Well, I was born of a small town whore, and my father was a man whore. I have been surrounded by sexual activity since age five, and have since learned that scientists tell us that while babies are still in the womb they know what is going on outside in the world and around them. They start learning before they are even born, which is how I started absorbing an appetite for sexual behavior so young. I am also guessing that my mom must have been a drug user and or a heavy drinker like my dad, but more about this later in my story.

One day when I woke up, half the building across the street from us had burned out. When I saw it, I thought, *What the hell? When did this happen?* I didn't hear a thing.

I don't recall the name of the man who lived there, but I do know that he and I had had sex a few times - or let's be realistic, I should say he was abusing me, given my young age. Even though I already wanted it, as he was a handsome man. A week later, after the building had burned down, I went through the back alley and saw a door that was half burned and had orange Police tape that said: Danger -- Keep Out. But the door was somewhat open, and I wanted to see what had happened inside, so I went up the stairway. It was dirty and smelled of charred wood.

When I got up to this man's apartment, I walked in and saw that nearly all of its contents were burned, melted, messy, and charred. As I was looking around the bedroom where he abused me I saw a partly-burned dresser whose contents had been spilled all over the floor. I spotted a bunch of magazines, including a few undamaged ones. The one I first saw had a picture of a beautiful, naked young boy around my age. My heart started pumping as I picked it up, and when I opened it, every picture was like that – winsome, lovely adolescent males my age, having sex. I sat on the dirty floor and couldn't stop looking at those pictures. I was mesmerized – shocked, yet relieved at the same time. I was so happy to see this printed evidence that there were other people like me. I wanted to scream and tell everyone about it. I took the few magazines that were not burned and hid them underneath my T-shirt, nervous as hell. I ran home, my heart still pounding, not wanting anyone to catch me with them.

Back in my bedroom, I spent hours looking at them, amazed, still in shock! I knew how to read only a bit, but now wanted so badly to know more about what the printed words in the magazines with those glorious, erotic images, said! I just kept trying to decipher all those mysterious printed words. I myself had been doing everything shown in those magazines with many guys, of various ages. I was able to make out that all the boys in the pictures were in California. I had no idea where California was, but I immediately knew that I wanted to go there.

I looked at these magazines for months till the pages were dog eared, taking care to hide them where my father wouldn't find them – a terrifying thought, given his propensity for violence. Those magazine became my Horny Bible, from which I discovered that I was a gay boy, and that this man was a gay man who liked having sex with young boys – a "pederast." Chancing upon these magazines relieved my confusion, and confirmed that there was a place for me in this world.

Before seeing them, I had not felt there was "a place" for me. I had instead sensed that everyone and everything around me was different, hostile and dangerous. I wish I could better explain what I was feeling, but perhaps one just had to have been in my shoes to understand what a comforting revelation this was for me. But I am sure that any gay guy who is reading this can relate to it.

These magazines were all about sex, showing green trees, dirt roads, hills and cute boys galore, engaging in every pleasure of the flesh males can experience, or share. I just couldn't believe what I was seeing and I wanted desperately to run to this paradise of "California," not knowing that it was just the artificial imagery of porn magazines. Despite all the dark corners of life I had been in, I was still young, and very naïve.

This was when I finally understood why I was always looking at sexy men and boys. I will write a lot about handsome men in upcoming chapters but until my discovery of those magazines in a burned out apartment, I didn't really understand the basis of my attraction to such men, or that it had a name.

I now grasped, at age 13, that what appeared in these magazines was the life I craved, and would do so throughout my whole life. Even today (in middle age, as I write), when I see a pretty face or a handsome man, I melt! And after the horrible bad luck of an abused childhood, I've been very lucky in that every straight or married man and gay guy I've been with - and I mean every one of them - has been extremely, and continue to be, immensely attractive! I don't mean to sound shallow or boastful, but that's just the way it happened and keeps happening. The Fate that made sex a nightmare for me as a child has compensated by making it a fabulous dream as an adult.

I have never really understood how I keep attracting such a crop of splendid men. I never felt like I was attractive. In fact, I always felt dirty and not worthy of anything, like I had been holding back a sordid secret that no one else must ever know. Because they would just push me away, and when we had sex they would take my love away.

I have been living with this puzzling impression for forty five years, but can finally let it all out! Indeed, I am starting to feel like I am cleansing my soul. My best friend, Franco would always tell me, "Carrino, how do you get all those hot guys? Every time I see you with a different guy, he is like the hottest guy in the bar or wherever we are."

I often ask myself that same question. Perhaps the answer isn't in my physical appearance. Could it be that the light that kept me going through all the darkness in my life shines so that others can see it now?

Let's remember the importance of expressing our appreciation to close family members, family harmony is the foundation for happiness and wellspring of the flourishing of our communities. **Daisaku Ikada.**

CHAPTER 6

AROUND THIS TIME, MY FATHER and I had moved from the apartment on Wicker Park and Wood Street. My Aunt Rosa moved to Milwaukee Avenue and Wood Street. By that time I was already a totally different kid from the one my Aunt Nivia had raised for two years.

I was in another, sort of "twilight zone." I started not trusting people and hated everybody including my family and my cousins. I would hang out with them and the family, but always kept a veil over my personality so they wouldn't see the real me. They would try to give me advice, but I would just look at them with this pain in me. My attitude was 'you were not there to protect me when I most needed it.' But how could they have, if they never knew what was going on with me?

I spoke ill of just about everyone, laughed at people, talked back to adults. I used to want to jump on people and literally rip off their faces. Filled with rage, I was jealous of kids who had real families. I started to hate my father even more than I already did. I always had this anger in me, but just couldn't let it out, because I was too scared, or too shy. The only way I knew to deal with people was by letting grown men use me sexually. I used to tell them, "Please give it to me," and that would make me happy for a moment - till the next one came along.

Once my family moved, all these new faces started popping up, my cousins, friends, etc. I started hanging with them, but mainly because there were also a lot of boys in their circle, who kept getting my attention. I did have sex with a lot of them, but I remember one of them especially, the hottest one in the whole group. All the girls in school wanted him, and out of school he was wanted anywhere he went. He was so steamy! Dark soft skin, beautiful full dark brown hair, great body, bedroom eyes, just the total package. He often wore corduroy pants that fit him tightly, and were somewhat worn out. I couldn't stop looking at him, especially at his bulging crotch. It looked so sensual, it would make me nervous just looking at it, like a starving kid who needed to eat. I just wanted to grab it and tell him to take me, but there were always lots of other kids around, so I would just stand back away from everyone and pretend that I was not looking. To protect his privacy, I won't include his name, but will call him EB, for "el bello" – the beautiful one.

One day, we were all playing hide and seek, and EB decided to come hide with me. We hid underneath a truck, at the A&P supermarket on Milwaukee and Wood Street. So there we were, underneath this huge truck and he got very close to me, close enough for me to grab his cock and start playing with it – which I did. When he didn't object right away I said, "You want to do me?"

He said, "Yes." I pulled his zipper down, and we had an intense encounter, right under that truck. When we were done, we came out all dirty and sweaty. We went back to the game and I felt powerful as I looked at all the girls, thinking, I have been with him, he loves me and not you. After that he and I had sex a few different times at his mother's place, and at my father's. This sort of episode was fairly typical for me at this time. Here I was, twelve years old, going on thirteen, totally out of control, but no one even seemed to notice it, especially my dad.

He started having poker games at his apartment, so all these older, handsome men would be coming over to play, getting drunk and loud. I used to stay in my room, sit on the stairs outside, or in the back of the building, sometimes till two or three in the morning. Sometimes, some of these men would take a break from cards, and go outside to stretch. I started noticing some of them I liked, so I would write suggestions on a tiny piece of paper, like, "you want me? I want to …." and it would always be some obscene proposal. I would give it to them, then sort of run away - but not too far, and I did this with a few of them. The first one to accept told me to touch his penis and play with him; we ended up having oral sex. The second one told me, "Not now, I will be over tomorrow when your dad is at the bar." So this also was a way for me to start asking men to seduce me by handing them what used to be called "mash notes."

Around this time, I came home from school one day and found this lady named Cuca had actually moved in during the time I'd been out. My father didn't even tell me in advance or get me ready for this any other way. It seems that this lady had fallen head over heels in love with my father, and she started being very wife-like, and trying to be motherly to me. But little did she know what she just got herself into! I stared at her with this hateful gaze. I never gave her a chance to really be nice to me, I simply made her life miserable from day one. I knew she wasn't going to be around long enough to really love me, and even if she were, she would then just end up leaving like the rest of my father's women.

She started moving things around and redecorating, and this made me especially mad, because I felt that such matters were my exclusive "thing." I made that place look the way it was, so every time I came home from school and she had done something, I would immediately put it right back where it had been. I started yelling, "*Bitch, tu eres una puta!*" which means, "You are a whore." "Don't touch my stuff!" I would warn her, but she kept putting it back where she wanted it. This went on for a few weeks, until one day I jumped on top of her and started furiously biting her, taking all my frustrations out on her. The look on her face said, 'What the hell is wrong with you? Ok, ok, I won't touch anything again!'

Sure enough, a month later she was gone. But before she left, my father used to beat the crap out of her. I actually used to stand in my bedroom doorway and see him punch her hard in the face. I could hear the bum-bum-bum every time he struck her. There was blood all over the place, ripped clothes and arguing. This happened at least four to five times in the morning, in the middle of the night, etc. I never did know why he beat her, I was too scared to ask, and maybe get a beating myself. But since I was so filled with hate then, I just assumed she deserved it.

A few months later, more new faces showed up, my father's new girl, Irma, her mother and her two kids. I got home just in time to see them bringing in their stuff in boxes, as they were taking all my stuff out of my room. The woman told me that this was going to be her kids' room now. My room was going to be upstairs on the second floor, in an apartment in the back of the building. My father just looked at me and told me these were going to be my new "little brothers" and new family, and he was helping them move in. He offered no explanations, no apologies for upsetting my life, nothing! He just shoved me upstairs, with only a bed, a kitchen table and my clothes. I was numb, scared, nervous, and filled with even more fury. So there I was in a semi-abandoned space, with no TV, no radio, nothing. I was alone in a beat up, mostly empty dump, with nothing but my rage to keep me company. I felt so left out and even less loved – if that was possible.

So as time passed, she, her kids and I all became combatants with each other! I made sure that they felt my hatred and fury. I used to come through the apartment and start throwing things down and knocking them over. They would ask me to throw out the garbage, but instead I would empty it onto the kitchen table while there was food there or her kids were eating on it. I hated her kids and her, and more than any of them, my father who was either never around, or sleeping. It got to the point that I eventually stopped coming down to the apartment. I would just go upstairs and hardly ever saw them. I would come home from school and find a plate of food for me in front of the door, like I was a dog or some other animal.

But it turned out that living there alone was like finding a new freedom. I started fixing up my pitiful little space, made it look somewhat nice, and turned it, pretty much, into a whorehouse. I had lots of men and boys coming through the back window next to the long stairs up to my room. I had men of all colors and sizes, sometimes as many as 12 to 15 guys a week coming into my own cramped little paradise. Often, it was one fellow right after another; while one man was in the shower, another one might be in the bedroom with his pants down while I was felating him. As soon as one left, I had another one having sex with me. And through all this, I never saw my father but just once. He came up to tell me to be nice to his girlfriend's kids. He didn't even walk into my apartment, just knocked on the door, told me to behave, and left. Little did he know that I had a guy hiding in the room at that very moment. And sex was only part of it. I had guys come over and get high, drunk, shoot up - you name it, and it was going on there. It was like I was back in that awful neighborhood in New York again, with all the drug activities.

A few months later - well yes, you guessed, it my father's latest lady and her kids were gone. She couldn't stand me, and my father would come home drunk every night. He would just sleep all day long, wake up and leave for work. Moreover, they argued like cats and dogs.

Right after that happened, my father decided to move to a different apartment not far away, Ashland and Palmer Street, in a corner apartment on the second floor. A new 'hood, a new adventure, and a new school for me. I already had turned 13 by this time, and puberty was starting to seriously kick in for me. Our new apartment was a pretty big place, with three bedrooms, and the building was somewhat like our previous one. There were four units, two in front and two in back, with a storefront right downstairs. So I fixed up our unit, painted it and made it as nice as I could.

When we lived there, I virtually never saw my dad. He came home from work at the bar drunk and just slept during most of each day. When I would get up in the mornings to go to school, the kitchen smelled like booze from his breath. I would make my breakfast, get ready and leave to go to Wells High, my new school.

This school was the worst of the worst I ever attended, and that's really saying something, a true dump, and a very dangerous one. Back then, all the kids there were completely out of control, fighting, carrying knives and guns, beating up teachers, breaking their car windows - the police came around all the time. Right away I started skipping class, doing whatever I could to avoid school. I would wait until I knew my father was leaving in the afternoon for his job, and pretend I had just gotten back from school. Since he never really talked to me (not once!), he never was aware of all this. My father and I never had a full conversation. It was more like

My Dad Looks like he is getting ready for bed after his night out working at the bar. The long beard, he had made a promise to let it grow for a year, I never did find out what the promise was.

"here are the food stamps" or he would just leave them on top of the table for me. He never would say, "Hi son, how are you today? How was school? Can I help you with your homework?" He never said anything to me. I sometimes came in and walked right in front of him, and it was like he was just another piece of furniture.

I'm sorry if it sounds monotonous when I talk about how indifferent, insensitive, selfish and generally terrible my father was, in terms of his duties as a parent. But I keep including this to remind you, the reader, of what I was up against in life. A mother who literally left me for dead, and a father who regarded me as a burden he resented, to whom he gave as little effort and attention as he could possibly manage. It's ironic actually, that parenthood is the most important task most people will ever have, but society provides no formal training for it. People need a license to show they know how to drive, but no proof at all that they are fit to have children. My own childhood is proof of what can happen when something so immeasurably important is just left to chance.

After a month or so of living here, he had been seeing a new girlfriend who owned the bar and building where he was working. She had six kids, so he took me over there one day, telling me, "Get in the car, we are going to go see a friend of mine." He didn't speak to me in the car or try to tell me, "This is what's going on, son." Nothing.

When we got to her house, I found that it was a badly decorated apartment with an old-fashioned '70s look, and all her kids running around. He immediately hugged and kissed her, and told me to go play with my "new brothers." My mind went blank at that moment, like, what the heck? I just went and sat on a beat up chair, while feeling very hurt inside. I was done and sick of this sort of crap! It was suddenly obvious that my father just expected me to serve as a baby-sitter to these strangers. It never crossed his mind that, perhaps, I didn't want to do that, or shouldn't have so much responsibility dumped on me when I was still little more than a child myself. Dad and his puta left me there alone, with these kids for me to take care of while they went downstairs to go work at her bar. But having not been consulted, I did no such thing; I just let those kids do whatever the hell they wanted, like I didn't give a damn what happened to them – because, frankly, I didn't!

Finally, my "new brothers" just passed out, sleeping all over the place. It was late now, and I wanted to go home. I went downstairs through the back door of the bar, and could see all the patrons dancing, playing pool, making out, sniffing cocaine, happy, laughing and generally having a great time. And from far away, where I was kind of hiding by the back door, I saw my father smoking, dancing, happy, hugging his new lady whom I had just learned about for the first time. I saw how he treated her, and felt terribly wounded, my eyes tearing up, like I just wanted to burst out crying! I was thinking, *how come he's never been like that with me?* I had never seen my dad so happy. He was always serious whenever he talked to me. So to me, this jolly lover-boy was a total stranger to me, as in "Who in the hell is this guy?!"

I went back upstairs and lay down around these kids on the sofa, and just started crying, asking God why? "Why? Are you doing this to me, God? Why am I like this? Where is my mother, why is she not coming to pick me up? When can I go home? I just want to go home to Abuelita, my grandmother. Please give me a sign, tell me something. I can hear you, please talk to me!"

I just fell asleep crying in this stranger's home suffocating in my own anger. It started to become the type of anger that was nasty, mean, hurtful like - I wanted to just wound somebody. But instead, I always ended up hurting myself, and having sex with any dude who wanted me.

I eventually woke up, and this lady, Juanita, told me come get ready and jump in the bathtub with my new little brothers. "I am going to take care of you from now on. I am going to be your new mom. Your dad is sleeping. He had a long night." I just looked at her and started crying. She said, "Oh no you don't, not around here, around here you do what I say!" She grabbed me by my arm and tried to pull me over to the bathroom, and I immediately sank my teeth into her hand, hard like a dog with rabies, just wanting to rip her skin off. She started screaming. "Angel, Angel, come help me, your son won't let go of my hand, and he's biting me hard!"

I bit her so hard that there was blood coming out of my mouth. Finally, my father ran into the room and started slapping me around and telling me, "How dare you! I didn't raise you like that! Get dressed! I am taking you home." Needless to say, it didn't occur to him to wonder why I was so upset – or to care that I was.

He didn't raise me to be like that? He didn't "raise me" at all! I was more of a nuisance to him than anything else, and if there'd been any doubt of that before, there no longer was. He looked on me as a sort of unpaid servant.

When we got to our apartment, he told me, "You need to behave, because she is moving in with us and that's why we moved here to a bigger place." Then he just simply went to his room and went to sleep. By this time I was like a ball full of nerves, shaking all the time and constantly jumpy, waiting for that next slap or other abuse, which experience had taught me was coming my way.

By this time, my father had repeatedly upset my life for his own benefit, without the least thought for how it might impact me, let alone asking for my input. This, along with all the other dangers and hostility I had faced since early childhood, had left me an absolute cauldron of nerves, always expecting some new blow or other abuse. But by this time, I was approaching adolescence, and decided I simply could no longer stand still and wait for the next misfortune a cruel Fate would amuse itself by hurling at me. I didn't want to be a nursemaid to these strangers. Also, my father's choice of sex partners had often been terrible for me, as they resented, mistreated and exploited me. But again, he never seems to have thought about what he owed me, even once.

Try to imagine what being treated that way for your whole childhood could do to your self-image, and view of life.

So I decided to leave my father's home that night, and never return if I could help it. Later that same day, after he came home from work and fell into a deep, snoring sleep, I went through his pants on the nightstand, and took every cent of money he had in them. Then, shaking like an earthquake with fear, yet with the courage of desperation, I ran out the door, down the stairs, and out of his life – free at last!

I never looked back, and don't know whether or not he actually bothered to look for me. It didn't matter to me, because the only thing that did register with me was that I was free of him, his cruelty, his selfishness, and his neglect. However, about six months later, a friend's mother insisted that I call my dad, just to let him know I was okay. I could have told her that he'd never cared about whether I was "okay" before, and probably only cared now because I'd taken his money, and left him without a babysitter. But to please her, I called him, and when he answered, I said, "Hi, it's me, and I left because I am a faggot!" Then I hung up, and didn't speak to him again for several months.

Bolting out of my father's house like that might seem rash, or excessive to some people, but it was the only way my 13-year old mind (with no adult to advise me) could see to shatter the cycle of fear and mistreatment that had been my life so far. It was an "extreme" action, but it was an "extreme" situation. I couldn't cope with it anymore, and feared I would lose my mind or my life if I didn't escape from it.

And this was when another extremely important page in my life turned. I had already met a few people in the vicinity of Dad's new apartment. One of them, Pedro, happened to be gay, the first openly gay person I'd ever met. So after creeping out of my dad's apartment, I ran to his place and started hanging out there, without telling him that I'd "run away" (though at my age, 13, this was not the act of a child who didn't really understand the implications of such an action) and that I had nowhere else to go. So I sort of moved myself in, sleeping over at his place and helping him with the household chores. He was super pleased with me helping him out, and eventually he realized I had nowhere else to go. I had brought no clothes with me and didn't have anything but the $88 I took from my dad. Since Pedro was just a few years older than me, we really got along together. He had left home around age fifteen or so, too. He also had the same type of life I did, that is, an abusive, non-supportive family. It was like a match made in heaven (in more ways than similar backgrounds, as I will explain below).

It's important to point out that he and I never had sex. Our relationship was more just friendship, and we became very close, in a way I never did with men who simply used me to gratify their appetites. He started giving me clothes, feeding me, etc. But the main, really critical thing I didn't know about him was that he supported himself by selling drugs. While living there, I would see people knock on his door at all times of the day and night, until I picked up what was going on (which happened quickly, because I'd seen this activity before in both Chicago and New York).

So I offered to help him with his drug trade. "Can I help you? Just tell me what to do." Very soon, I was all over the area, making deliveries for him, and helping him arrange all the parties he would have. He had a party just about every weekend, his apartment teeming with hot guys. I had never seen so many overtly gay men in my life; there was writhing sex in every corner of Pedro's apartment, and I thought I was in heaven. Pedro and I would let all these guys just take turns on us. This is when I learned what an orgy was, and believe me, I was involved in all of them.

I learned so much about gay life with him: He would tell me what to look for and who not to look at, but I already was somewhat of an expert on such matters without even knowing it. All I knew was that I felt safe and (for the first time) at ease there, being around people who were like me. And just for the record, I must point out that, at that time, I also met a lot of decent guys who were gay and were not like us – that is, drug-selling male sluts. They were more educated, and monogamous. Some went to school, others lived with their parents, were loved by them, and loved them back. For me – with a family that, for the most part, treated me horribly (criminally so, I now realize), hearing about lives like these guys was like discovering a totally different world. I wanted to be more like them, but didn't know how or where to start. I didn't think that I was worthy of such in idyllic life. I feared I was already so damaged that I couldn't be fixed. Try to imagine what it would be like to realize such a thing when you were 13, old enough to have good reason to fear that, with most of your life yet to live, but thinking you were probably past saving.

I lived with Pedro till I was 15 and during those two years, I was usually surrounded by no one but gangbangers, drug dealers, a few Mafia types. My "routine" included lots of sex, fights, guns going off, people beating each other, fighting over drugs and drive-by shootings.

Also, Pedro moved a lot. He had to, to avoid getting caught with all the drug dealing he had going on, not to mention all his drug-heavy "parties" he gave. But wherever he moved, he always made sure I had a place to sleep there. One of his apartments had a door in the living room that he kept secret, by covering it with a huge rug. It led to the basement, where they stored huge blocks of cocaine and marijuana. He had kids from the 'hood working down there, mixing and packing the stuff to get it ready to sell. My job was to stay by the kitchen door, and when someone knocked on it, I was to ask what they wanted, take their money and hand them their drugs through a hole in the door, like for a mail slot.

Still a kid, I thought I had it made in such a situation; despite its crime, violence and danger, it was indescribably better than what my life had been before, because it provided me some actual enjoyment – unknown to me. I had somewhere to live, food, Pedro's hand-me-down stylish clothes, a few bucks in my pocket, and all the sex I wanted from the beautiful boys who would come over to get high and party. By this time I was already getting high myself to help me numb the bitterness of my previous life, and forget about it for a while. But in reality, taking drugs that way just made me feel worse; there were times that the drugs would affect me, and make

Age 12 One of my first
Public Schools Picture

me start thinking about my life and just start crying uncontrollably. I felt filthier than ever before, if that was possible. But I just figured, well, this is what my life is supposed to be like, so I would just keep doing it, letting guys have sex with me and drugging myself into rhapsodic oblivion. The mixture of the two experiences just seemed to work for me somehow, and made me "happy". Or at least that's what I thought. It's a basic instinct to crave immediate, sensory gratification. I was certainly doing that, so by that measure, my life was happy. Only, of course, it really wasn't. It was, as I'd said, just numbed.

Pedro's grandmother lived right next door to him, and she was a bigger drug dealer than he was. Everyone in the neighborhood loved her, especially if you were going to buy drugs. She was a nice lady though, but serious. Kind of like the "Godfather," everyone used to kiss her hand, then she would bless them. She was especially nice to me since I lived with Pedro. She treated me like a family member, served me food, and gave me marijuana. She would always ask me if I needed anything and if I was ok. I think she noticed that I really didn't fit in with this sort of crowd, since I was more of a shy, scared, quiet, loner type of kid. I didn't have a truly mean bone in me; all the times I've described when I swore or lashed out at other people were not due to my being "mean," but to my being scared, hurt and angry – not to being mean. I was soft, afraid, and wouldn't pick fights with anyone. Everyone else around there did, but they would always look out for me, so no one would harm me. It was like they really liked me a lot, and since I had so rarely felt that kind of care before, when these people just showed me a little love. I was hooked! I felt like these people loved me. They may have been drug dealers and users, but they were far kinder to me than most of my family ever were, especially my parents, who should have been the kindest of all. In my case, it was just the opposite.

Then, one day Pedro's grandmother's house got raided. It was a huge operation; there were police and dogs everywhere. They taped her house shut, so no one could go in. They put her and a few others in handcuffs, just like in the movies, then started dragging out huge blocks of marijuana. I have no idea where in the hell she had all that stuff hidden, because I had never seen it when I came over to her place. It had been wonderful feeling the love I'd gotten there, but this situation really scared the hell out of me, as it could have landed me in very serious trouble with the law myself. I didn't want to go to jail, so I had to get the hell out of my dependence on Pedro, and in the back of my mind, I started thinking about those gay guys who were more clean and decent than any I had met before. Those guys showed me that gay life could be more than crime, violence and instability.

But I didn't know where to go, and didn't want to let Pedro down, when he had been so good to me. Luckily for me however, Pedro had run out of his stock of drugs when they raided his grandma's house, but people kept coming over to buy stuff from him. Besides, no one wanted to be near that place for a while. In desperation, Pedro started packaging sugar as if it were cocaine, and began selling it to his customers for a few days. When they realized what he was doing, they started looking for him to beat him up and maybe kill him. So with the money he had made, he bought a plane ticket and fled to L.A.

After that, he was gone from my life as suddenly as he had entered it, and I never heard from him again till many years later. He really was not a bad guy, but he is still stuck in the '70s, so I just say hi and bye any time I see him. So I want to take this occasion to say, Thanks Pedro for being in my life at the time when we really needed each other.

With Pedro's hasty departure, I was suddenly homeless again. But when I was selling drugs for Pedro, I met a bunch of prostitutes who used to buy from me, and I went to their apartments and asked them if I could stay with them because I had nowhere else to go. Since I was so nice to them, they agreed to let me stay. They all lived in an apartment building that was almost falling apart, hiding away in a corner nearby. It was a filthy, spooky place, so of course I started cleaning, doing their laundry and cooking for them. To them, such courtesies were a big deal and they loved it. And they really needed my help, as they were utter pigs! Living with these women was like living in a garbage can. I didn't stay there too long, because I started getting scared of their pimps, who would come over and beat the crap out of them. This used to remind me too much of my father, so I just disappeared.

So at this point I became homeless again. However, I remembered some of the people at a gay bar called The Factory back then, where I used to stand outside to sell drugs to many of the customers. I became friends with a few of them, mostly drag queens, and most of them, whores as well. I didn't care, because they were really good to me. I was too young to get into the bar, so I started waiting outside, for example letting them know if there were policemen coming while they were turning tricks. In return, they would give me a few dollars here and there, and when the bar closed, I used to tag along with them since I had nowhere else to go. At that point, I just had a backpack and a few things to carry with me wherever I went. I stayed with anyone who would let me spend the night. Occasionally, I would also go home with tricks I started meeting on my own, and let them have sex with me just for a place to sleep.

I kept living like this until I was around 17. With no real home, I was always waiting for that glorious moment when I would be magically whisked back home to Puerto Rico, still hoping for my mother to show up someday and take me with her. Even though I knew, rationally, that it was not going to happen, expecting it gave me hope somehow - and if there is one thing I have learned from my life, it's that people need hope as much as we need food and shelter. Such was my faith that, from the age of 14 to 17, every Mother's Day, I would buy a Mother's Day card just in case she showed up. And every time, when she failed to do so, I would just cry by myself somewhere where no one would see me, then angrily rip the wasted card apart.

Devastated and heartbroken, I would look into the sky and ask God why these terrible things – which I couldn't imagine I'd done anything to deserve – were happening to me. "Why have you forgotten me? What have I done? Why me? Please help me, show me what I need to do so I can go home. I'm sorry, I didn't mean to be bad, so please forgive me. You seem to forgive everyone else, but not me. Why?" I would ask as I would sit there alone, crying till my eyes seemed to float, and talking to the empty sky. Eventually, I had some of the people I was hanging with get me a fake ID so I could get into the bars. Back then, all you needed was a birth certificate and voila, you were admitted. The first time I entered a gay bar as a customer, I was simply overjoyed! It was amazing, mobs of gay guys and drag queens dancing to frenzied music, the atmosphere lively, attractive people carrying on without any kind of restraint! Lines of people waited to get into the bathroom, where some would have sex, and some were doing cocaine. There were guys making out everywhere, glimpsed through the haze of cigarette smoke that taverns had at that time.

It was like I had died and went to heaven. Before I knew it, I was there, at the Factory, three or four times a week. I would walk there from wherever I lived. Snowstorms, rain, heat waves – nothing would stop me from going to this little patch of Paradise. I just wanted to be in this bar all the time. And since it was so easy for me to pick up men and have them take me to their homes, I made it my new base of operations. I never had money on me, but somehow I didn't need to. Guys and drag queens would always buy me drinks and get me high.

But when I started to drink and get high regularly, I turned into a different person, who wasn't shy at all. I felt powerful and in total control, and deep inside, this seemed to really help me forget about all the lousy things that had happened to me, and the fact that I still really had no place to live. It was like I just stepped into a fantasy world, which I stayed in for years. But the fantasy would disappear every morning after, every time I woke up in a different bed. All of a sudden, when the drugs and alcohol wore off, I became the shy teenager again, and would leave whoever's place I was in immediately, before they noticed who I really was. I usually felt stupid, but when I would get drunk, I just turned into a witty, talkative youth. It was like Spiderman's story: wimpy by day, and in command by night. I have never been able to fully shake off this self-image, and still feel like that sometimes.

This day-night transformation was also part of my father's personality, which is why he almost never talked to me. He was angry by day, but was Mr. Big by night. Believe it or not, I am just realizing this similarity now, as I'm writing this book. As I do so, I keep telling myself, maybe I shouldn't reveal so many dreadful secrets. I don't want to hurt anyone, but I have been hurt far more than I should have been, and finally putting it in words is helping me gather all the missing puzzle pieces in my life, and start to make sense of them. So I will keep writing it.

I remember reading that Henry Ford was not very book smart, and had very little schooling, but persevered, and made himself one of the most remarkable men in history. Knowing that makes him an icons and inspirational for me. I read that Mr. Ford used to build upon other people's knowledge to do all of his work, and most of it was free. He used to get it from his friends, and at times paid for a specialist for his expertise.

Remembering Ford's approach, I started to use other people's knowledge to get along in life, but most often simply by watching them, more than by listening. I have never been able to be a great listener, even today, but am a terrific "watcher," and learn things very quickly this way. Gathering information by watching has enabled me to become a first-rate hair stylist, fashion expert, and to develop other parts of my personhood, of which I am proud.

Also, if it weren't for my ghostwriter's writing skills, I wouldn't have been able to articulate my experiences for this book properly. It didn't come free, but I am (despite my teenaged impression that I was not) smart enough to be able to buy his assistance. Further, by using my friend Brad's editing skill to follow up my "ghost," I was also able to accomplish a lot of these things I have done. I was able to organize my thoughts better, and thus describe my experiences more clearly. Sometimes he helps me for free, and sometimes I just exchange his talent for mine by cutting his hair, and a lot of times I paid him. He's the one who is actually helping me edit this book, and in return I will cut his hair till I am done writing and publishing it. Believe me when I tell you that I can hardly spell, but thanks to new technology, every time I don't know how to spell a word, I simply click a button and voila! Spelling options appear on my screen, one of which is always the one I want. And thanks to my ghost's skill, between us, I was able to put my story together in a coherent form that people who don't know me can follow.

My point here is that I was really never as stupid as I thought I was – my talents just lay in areas that weren't always the ones our society values most. Grasping this made me want to be a better person and set a goal for myself, but before I started using this realization properly my life just kept getting more confusing and chaotic.

So returning to the story of my late teens, by going to the Factory all the time and meeting all sorts of people (not all of them savory) there, I was on the edge of tumbling down an abyss to a life wasted by sensual excess. I was using drugs, was using people, and was sleeping with anything that had male equipment attached - as long as it also had a pretty face. Soon I was helping people steal stuff, assisting with break-ins. I almost started prostituting myself, but didn't - not for money at least.

During this period, I met two exceptionally attractive guys, George and Tony, whose physical beauty was literally arresting – they would stop viewers in their tracks. I started hanging out with them, and we would have sex in Tony's car, or each one would take turns with me in the back seat, while the other drove. They were genuine hustlers, of the worst kind. They would steal people's wallets, coats, bikes, gasoline (with a hose) and anything else of use or value that they could get hold of.

They would go to the Gold Coast, Chicago's richest area, where wealthy men would go to pick up guys by driving around in a park, and set them up for burglaries. Either George or Tony would get picked up, arrange to go to his client's home (which was usually nearby), get their address, and then ask if the client (called a "trick") could wait a minute, so George or Tony could tell a friend where he was going. Tony or George would then come and tell the other guy and me the trick's address. After getting there, as soon as the trick wasn't looking, George or Tony would go and unlock his front door, then take the trick to the bedroom. Then we were to wait a few minutes while George or Tony got the trick distracted with sex. They had this process all timed out; George or Tony and I would go in through the unlocked door, and rummage through the guy's apartment, stealing whatever we could carry in our pockets. It was mostly money, and before whoever was with the trick left, they would also steal the guy's wallet, unless we had found it first. I remember running like hell away from such scenes, back to their car.

We would all hide in the back seat until it was safe to drive away, then go to a new destination and do it all over again.

One day, it was my turn to go with the trick a much older man. I was so nervous and shaky that he looked at me and asked what was wrong and I told him I was just cold. He went into the bedroom and got naked. I lied to him, telling him I had to go to the bathroom. On my way there, I unlocked the front door. George and Tony were literally right outside it. They walked in and pushed me toward the bedroom. I was standing there, looking at this old guy, and just couldn't get myself to touch him, being only used to attractive men, which he certainly was not. Suddenly, I heard the front door slam; the old man heard it too and right away realized what was going on. He screamed, "You fucking little bastards! I am going to fucking shoot you!"

I bolted for the door, and was already halfway out when Tony grabbed me by my arm and started running, with me following as fast as I could. Jumping down the exit stairs two at a time, we reached the building's back alley and dashed to the car. We all threw ourselves on top of each other to hide laughing our asses off, like the whole episode was fun. That was the most intense experience for me with George and Tony's capers. In the back of my mind I knew this was not right, but my anger at life was more powerful than any sense of guilt. I just kept thinking, *they need to suffer like I suffered.*

As things turned out, I was saved at the very edge of the chasm of living my whole life as a drugged out, thieving whore by my friend Dan. He never knew when he first met me, but saved me, without knowing it, from a life of crime, certain prison, and possible early death. If it weren't for him, I would be writing this book from jail with Tony and George – if at all.

I always looked up to Dan, and he taught me something that has always stayed with me: "Rose, if you're going to be gay, be the best gay that you can be." He calls me Rose even to this day, because back then, I was a huge fan of the Bette Midler movie, *The Rose.* I even dressed in drag a few times and called myself Rose. And even though I have had many ups and downs, whenever I try to achieve something, fail, and get depressed, 'what a failure I am. I'm never going to be anyone special,' I would ask myself, what would Dan have done? Then I would brush myself off, look forward and try again. I have never tried so many different ways of achieving something memorable, something that would give me that 15 minutes of fame. I am still trying. It's like an addiction for me. I must, and will, achieve my dream. At the end of this book, I will talk more about all the lovely rainbows I have pursued.

When I was 18, Dan gave me a ticket to fly to Puerto Rico for vacation, and I went with my best friend Linda, Linda was my best friend the one who defend me and protect me like a hawk from everyone and anyone who tried to hurt me or make fun of me she was my Tomboy girlfriend, I was more feminine than her we also lived with Pedro together for a while, I used to listen to her Mom's advice and always took it to heart throughout my teenage years. I respected her and how she was raising her 4 kids who have turned out to be very sweet kind adults I like to say, "Thank you to Miriam for being there for me and all your great advice that did come very useful throughout my teenage years and to my darling friend Linda for always being there for me when I was scared and frightened and always made me feel saved. Linda's family gave us somewhere to stay. After our vacation, Linda went back home to the U.S., but I decided to stay in Puerto Rico. I wasn't going to give up the chance to go home – by which I meant my grandmother's house, the last place I even felt safe and loved, more than a dozen years earlier -so I started my search, remembering little things of where I had once lived and eventually found my way to her old house.

When I got there, its appearance was a total shock. The cute little house my grandma had raised me in was a disaster zone. It looked like it had been abandoned for years, even though my uncle was still living there. I reached the gate and called out to my gay uncle, "Manolin." He came out to the old door screen, looked out, and I asked him, "Do you remember me?"

He quickly said, "Yes of course, you're Hector. You look just like your mother. What are you doing here? When did you get here, and how?"

So I told him I was coming home, and he just looked at me in astonishment. I knew he didn't know what to say. So, he asked me to come in. When I walked inside, my heart just sank. The inside was even worse than the outside; the place looked like bums lived there. He showed me my old bedroom, which now seemed scary and unpleasantly empty. So many memories there. And now abandoned across from it was the room where I played with Joey. I was looking at all this and had flashbacks and immediately knew, I have to get the hell out of this place. Also, I couldn't stand the smell.

Uncle Manolin and I became very close. He told me all the horrible things that had happened to me in early childhood, before I had any memories (or the ones I had were too indistinct – and often ghastly – for me to understand). We started looking for my mom, but everywhere we went, we just kept getting the same answer: "No, we have no idea who she is." I lived in Puerto Rico for roughly four years until I was about 21, and I never stopped looking. Sadly, I never did find her, and I have been emotionally homeless ever since.

My Uncle Manolin kept telling me, "I feel sorry for you." I disliked when he told me this, as it just made my anger stronger, though of course, he didn't mean it to hurt

Hector M Abreu

me. And he noticed that I was a little floozy who wanted to have sex with as many guys as he could. So one day, he told me that I was just like my mother; she would sleep with anybody, and I was doing exactly what she had done. That proves the power of heredity; I had never met her, yet was just like her? But even odder, Uncle Manolin was exactly like me and my dad (his brother), so could this just have been something that was already in my blood? Was it in me while I was still in my mother's womb? The abuse, the rape the molestation? What? And why? Even today, as an adult, I still don't understand it, and guess I never will.

But I found my solution (if not "the answer") to my plight when I became a Buddhist and started chanting, "Nam, myojo, renge, kyo," and learned all about the Buddhist beliefs that I still stand and live by today. That is that it's my karma to be in this sad, cheerless life, and to have lived through all this suffering and hurt, and that it's up to me to change my fate, and turn it around.

And this is exactly what I have done. Through my Buddhist practice, I have been able to connect all the loose wires lashing around in my life, and as time passes I keep connecting them. It has enabled me to find contentment and coherence in my world. I have my best friend Tony, who first introduced me to Buddhism, to thank for this. So Tony, wherever you are, I hope you're having a beautiful life, and thank you for showing me a way to cope with my anger and sense of having been wronged literally since birth.

But back to my story from before I found Buddhism. After I had been back in Puerto Rico for about four years, I met my first puppy love, Eddie. He and I were just head over heels in love with each other, but no matter how much affection someone showed me at this time, I just couldn't seem to stay faithful, sexually. I used to have sex with all his friends, and even strangers while he was away at school and work. Our relationship started falling apart about a year after it had begun. This was when my own frame of reference – of abusive relationships - started to cause problems for Eddie and me. After our first idyllic year, we spent three years of hell. I started treating him like what I had learned from my dad.

There is a universal, intelligent, life force that exists within everyone and everything. It resides within each one of us as a deep wisdom, an inner knowing.

Shakti Gawain

CHAPTER 7

WHEN I WAS LIVING WITH Eddie, I would go out, and wouldn't come back until the next day, carousing as I pleased. We would argue over anything, and he would discover me being intimate with other guys all the time. My vocabulary when speaking to him during those days was unprintable. It was like that wild 13-year old kid I had been never left. In fact, that kid has always been within me, throughout most of my life, really. I still, to this day, have him on my shoulder, I just have taught myself how to cope with the punk much better, and to know right from wrong.

I was 22 and had just moved to Chicago from Puerto Rico

My love for Eddie was a very needy, sick type of love, a bizarre combination of hatred and envy and jealousy, yet I was often very good to him at the same time. He had a family and a good job, a much more stable life than I had – though at the time I probably didn't even realize that I was envious. So my guess is that he stayed with me hoping that he could change me, since he obviously saw some good in me. Most important, he did help me find something to do with my life. He noticed how creative I was with anything I did, especially with blow-drying hair, so he enrolled me in a local beauty school. I was eighteen when I went to my first cosmetology school in

Santurces Rio Piedras, Puerto Rico. Prior to that, I didn't even know there was such a thing as a beauty school! "Beauty Academy," I think it was actually called.

There, I learned how to do hair but didn't learn a thing when it came time for theory. Teachers often told me, "Hector, you're a great hair stylist, but if you don't pass your board exams, you won't get your license to work legally." Well, apparently I never took learning seriously enough. I just went there because I made lots of women friends who really liked to hang out with me, which made me feel special. I was the best hair stylist there, so they learned a lot from me. You see, I have always learned how to do things visually (rather than by reading or listening). I taught myself to just watch how other people did things and then I would pick it up in a heartbeat.

So I finished the course but never passed the school exam, or even bothered to try. And once salon owners saw what I could do, I started getting job offers without a hair license; back then, the state authorities didn't really monitor the salons about licensed stylists (as they do nowadays).

But as I got older, I started to see the importance of having the license. So in 1984, at nearly age 23, worn out from my relationship with Eddie, I returned to Chicago, where I already had some family and a solid base of friends.

I went to Cannella Beauty School, but did exactly the same thing I did at my first school. I just didn't pay attention and couldn't learn anything unless it was visual. I took classes twice at Cannella's, but didn't pass either the school exam or apply for the state boards to get my stylist's license. The story of how I found the will to overcome my learning problems – and to become a highly skilled beauty professional – is very important, and I will return to it in depth later.

I reconnected with some of my Chicago friends from back when I was 17 and became a roommate with my best friend Gilbert whom I knew back when I was living on the streets in Chicago (may he rest in peace).

We rented an apartment that only cost $190 per month; that was cheap even for 1984, and it was an unspeakable dump! But between the two of us, we turned it into a beautiful sex palace. Even the landlord couldn't believe how splendid we made the place.

I lived with Gilbert for about two years, during which I started dating, and of course, sleeping with anyone who aroused me. But many of those guys didn't really want to be boyfriends, so in fact, my "relationships" always turned out enormously painful. I was like a sick child whose medicine was to want to be loved, so when the "therapy" didn't work, I would cry crushed tears of blood! I would make a fool of myself, begging my latest object of desire, "Please don't leave me! I have no one, you're the only one who has really showed affection, and who has cared for me," I would plead.

Some of these guys I just dated for a few weeks, others for a few months and here and there one would stay with me for a whole year or two. But I suffocated each and every one of them with my emotional excess. I was needy, shy, didn't know how to communicate well, and was pathologically jealous. I would spy on them and go through their personal stuff – I would even use witchcraft to try to win their love back again.

Mostly, though, I just would make myself look pathetic. Occasionally, when I was drunk at the bars, I would run into one of these former lovers, and create a huge drama, begging, in front of people, "Please, please! I love you so much! I can't live without you, you're my world, you're all I have!"

And yes, I was this dramatic for years. I always kept telling myself that this is my father and mother's fault, which made me even angrier, internally. In any case, the reality of having so many toxic liaisons was that I didn't really know what true love was. I just thought it was to cook, clean, and spread my legs in bed for a "lover."

I did this for years and years for so many different men I can no longer even remember all their faces (let alone their names), until I was very mentally and emotionally damaged– in addition to being verbally and physically abused in most of these affairs. I also tested positive for HIV. And all this came after (and probably as a result of) the affection starvation of my childhood and adolescence.

There is a French word that describes most of the relationships during my young adulthood: "Mesallisance." It often means a bad partnership, people who come together for affection but are in fact hopelessly wrong for each other. The horrifying fact – which must have been obvious to everyone but me, at the time – was that, at that stage of my life, I was "hopelessly wrong" for anyone; what I was seeking could not be found in a true, healthy partnership.

One of my last affairs during this time was with a guy named Rafy. When I was 36, I had left Chicago, moved back to Puerto Rico and lived there for about a year or so. Then, when I decided to move to South Beach, in Florida, Rafy tagged along with me because, supposedly, he was madly in love with me. I wasn't in love with him, but I liked his company. He was fun to hang out with.

This situation turned out to be a foul brew of all my ex-boyfriends in one! I eventually ended up falling in love (so I thought) with Rafy and became that little housewife/boyfriend, again! I was so desperate for love- still at my age of thirty six to thirty eight - that I once more transformed into a writhing, repulsive mass of needy, devouring obsession. Not surprisingly, all this made Rafy fall "out of love" with me.

But this time was different from the cycle of lovers over the previous years. This time, the pain was truly profound, so deep that I maintained my crazed pursuit of Rafy (who had moved out of our apartment, and wanted nothing to do with me) for almost two years. It eventually got so bad that whenever I saw him at a bar, he would warn me to stay away from him, or he would have me thrown out.

Shortly after we moved to South Beach, Rafy had gotten to know just about everyone on the beach there. I didn't do that, because I was too busy being a stay at home wife, while he went out and roamed. He got a job at a bar, started not coming home, and telling me things like he'd gotten lost last night on his way home, I didn't have enough money for the bus, so I stayed at one of the bartender's apartments. One time Rafy showed up two days later with a dozen hickeys on his neck, and when I asked him about it, he told me that all the guys at the bar ganged up on him and gave him all those hickeys. Such is the power of denial that I blindly, stupidly trusted him and believed what he would tell me – because facing the truth was even more frightening. I began to realize how similar this was to how I myself had treated Eddie and lots of other people.

It turned out that he had already slept with almost all of South Beach, virtually in front of my face, yet I didn't see it happening! Or maybe my sickening variant of love didn't let me, or want me to see the truth? Where we lived, we had a neighbor named Manuel who became friends with me, and would get me high and drunk, then would ask me, "Why don't you go out and have fun, enjoy yourself; you're a handsome guy, go have fun!" He told me this many times. It happened that he had often seen Rafy making out with different guys; that's why he was so persistent with me to go enjoy myself. He knew that I didn't actually have a "lover."

One day, Rafy told me that our relationship was not working, and that he was moving out. I was beyond devastated – nearly comatose! My world turned dark gray that day. Once again, it was me on my knees, maniacally begging a man I had believed loved me (and whom I believed I loved) not to abandon me. I cried so much after that shock that I could have filled up a pool with my tears. To make matters worse, I had no one to turn to or to speak to, since he had turned all of our mutual friends in South Beach against me. Everybody who we had met together started to turn away from me.

Rafy came home one day bruised all over. I had no idea how he got that way, but he told people that I had beat him up, and so turned all of them against me. So I was not only abandoned, I was shunned – with real hostility – by a faithless liar who had poisoned all possible sources of emotional support for me, and whom, for some mad reason, I was anxious to keep in my life.

When Rafy moved out, he left me with nothing but a hotdog, an apple and a cup of rice. As a result of being HIV +, I had been receiving a small Social Security stipend, which I used to pay all the bills and rent, and all I asked him to do was to buy food. He hardly ever did so, since he would spend his checks on getting high and drinking. Thus, at least, I was not financially dependent on him.

So there I was in South Beach, alone in a barren apartment, no one to call, no one to hang out with, no one to reach out to (by this time, Manuel had moved away) - dumped, devastated, desperate. Everywhere I went in the area would remind me of him, and all I could do was sob. One time I cried so hard that I began suffocating. I was standing against the kitchen wall and crumpled to the floor, weeping until I fell asleep. When I woke up on the floor, I just started wailing again, feeling so stricken that I didn't belong in this world and that it (the world) was telling me I wasn't worthy of happiness. This cycle repeated for several days, then for about two months, I would take Tylenol PMs two or three times a day, to try to sleep through the pain.

Then eventually I started telling myself, "Hector, pull yourself together!" I was now starting to realize that I was not the center of the universe, so I started chanting. "Nam-Myogo_renge_kyo", which is a practice of my Buddhist belief. Chanting would make me feel like I was cleansing my soul, but trust me, I was like an open water faucet, weeping while I was chanting and during the rest of my waking hours.

But I kept chanting every day for about three months, for my happiness, for the right things to start happening in my life, to attract the right type of people, etc. Also, I started "putting myself out there" and meeting people. Most of them were mainly for sex, but I was also always looking for something more, for a real friend. Let me tell you: If you ever live in pleasure-oriented South Florida, finding a true friend is one rare thing to have happen, since it's mostly a party place. But regardless I kept trying. I kept meeting guys who just wanted to get laid, who would get me drunk and stoned. When I was younger, that was fun and sufficient, but by this stage of my life, it would make me feel like crap and I would start crying again in front of strangers. Needless to say, that was a huge turn off to someone who just wanted to have sex and party with me.

But Karma – or simply "what goes around comes around" – finally began to work for me, because eventually, everyone Rafy and I had known in the area got to see how horrible he really was and how much he had lied to all of them about anything and everything. In fact, it turned out that most of our whole relationship was based on lies. So all these people started coming around me again, which was one of the changes that began to turn my life around. This is when I met Edward, an older man who changed my life forever.

Ed was a South Florida rarity: He became a true friend. He shared everything with me; food, drinks, boys, etc.! He sincerely liked me just as a buddy (we were never intimate), and I liked him the same way. It was serendipitous that he too was a Buddhist, so sometimes we would chant together.

Ed noticed something that few other people (even in my family) ever had: I was always sad, both internally and externally (that is, both privately and visibly). The reason most people didn't notice this truth was because I was always "wearing my veil" – usually concealing my thoughts and feelings - that I had become so good at, since I was 13 years old or so. He saw through that veil, and noticed that I was always forcing myself to have fun – but lots of times he would see me crying, or with tears still clinging in my eyes. He knew what I went through, as I shared a lot of things with him. Since I was still pretty unfamiliar with South Beach and hadn't gone out very much, he started introducing me around, showing me how to get around, where to go, trying to help me snap out of my bleak situation. Until that one special day when he got tired of my complaining about Rafy and told me, "Hector, I think that you're the one with the problem, not Rafy. He's gone and moved on. I am sorry, hon, but really, you have a problem and you need therapy."

I was hurt at first when he said it, but the next day, at home, I started thinking about what Ed had told me, and asking myself, "Why am I the one with the problem, instead of Rafy?" And then I began to really think about my life, from when I was born up to that point, and realized that Ed was right! I finally understood why every relationship I was ever in ended the same way – in disappointment at best, or in disaster at worst.

Sometimes, when we start doing things a certain way, they come to seem "normal" to us, even when anyone else can tell that what we are doing is not normal – and even unhealthy and self-destructive. And that's what the horrible deficit of love I had experienced in childhood had done to me. But once I figured that out (thanks to Ed's tough love), I told myself that I would never do this sort of thing to myself again.

I started to put myself together, not "again," really, but for the first time. I started reading positive books like Shakti Gawain, Doctor Bernie Segal, motivational tapes, "Think and Grow Rich," etc. And I did a lot more chanting. I would go and have a workout on the beach every morning, then go into the sea for a quick swim. I found a barber's chair, turned my tiny kitchen into a salon and started cutting my friends' hair. I didn't make much money doing that, but it was enough to maybe buy myself an occasional slice of pizza. My patrons were more acquaintances than friends. I lived in South Beach for four years, but only made six true, loyal friends (all of whom I am still in touch with).

It was at this point that my life truly started turning around - and one day I met Roberto Maluta! An Italian man – the real thing, not an "Italian-American" - who was so blazing attractive that I simply couldn't believe how much that he adored me. Everyone would flirt with him right in front of my face, slip phone numbers in his back pocket, waiters would write down their numbers on the bills when he would pay for meals, etc. I mean everyone, even women would flirted with him. But Mr. Roberto really wanted only me; he totally fell in love with me, so much that he started coming to Florida from his home in Italy every other month, and gave me $25,000 so I could open a retail shop. We called it Little Italy and sold a lot of used Italian merchandise that he would ship to me or bring with him on his visits.

He treated me so wonderfully, but I'd been hurt so badly so often before that I couldn't help but ask myself, "Wait a minute, what's wrong with this picture?" Roberto would give me or buy me anything I wanted, just spoiled me for the almost two years that we were together. It was like a fantasy. He was the first man who ever treated me like I was a movie star. He made me feel special, like I belonged in this world, and he didn't care about any of my imperfections. He accepted me just the way I was.

Yes, you're right… there was a but! By the time I met him, I had built protective walls of steel around my heart. I did love him back, and treated him as well as he treated me. - we had so much fun together and often laughed for hours - but I kept telling myself all the time, "Hector, don't let those walls down. Love, but don't fall in love, really; don't go in deep." I kept remembering my agony with Rafy, when it was like my heart was crushed by a mountain and I have never entirely recuperated since. I still have that heart of steel - as anyone would, who had endured what I had.

However, as I said, I did stay with him for almost two years, and we keep in touch to this day. I tell him all the time that he was the best man I have ever met in my life; he tells me the same thing and calls me Bambino, which means Baby in Italian.

It has, overall, been a good thing that I have kept my heart unexposed; it was due to knowledge gained at a terrible cost. In any case, the store didn't do well, and we had to close it down. Also, he had lots of problems back in Italy, so I couldn't come live with him there. The last time I saw Roberto was when he came to visit me while I was in beauty school in Miami in 1998. He visited for two weeks, and I remember waving goodbye to him as he walked towards the airport. I knew then that it would be years before we'd see each other again, but I didn't suffer. I thought about him and missed him, but by then, I had developed the emotional strength to move on when it was necessary, rather than just dissolve. And like a responsible adult, I kept concentrating on my schoolwork.

I loved Roberto, but I never truly fell in love with him or anyone else for that matter until I met Adam. After him, I just kept meeting guys, having fun with them, and sleeping around. Many times, men have wanted to be in a relationship with me, but I would ask them, "Are you ready and willing to be in an open relationship?" Because that was a non-negotiable condition for me, and I was very honest about it. I did this for fifteen years or so, and no one could ever accept that condition. Telling people not to expect me to be completely committed to them was one of my "walls." I would never truly let anyone in to my deepest "self." I would date sporadically, but my heart walls would never come down. On the few occasions I found myself getting involved with someone, but we split up, I would get over it in a couple of hours. I made a stern promise to myself and kept it: I would never again hurt like I was hurt by Rafy.

Even worse was the fact that Rafy was so uniquely undeserving of such devotion – an ungrateful liar, and a callous slut who has probably played with other men's hearts as he toyed with mine. It's sad, really. Eventually, terrible things usually happen to people (and not just gay men) who act that way, and they are often completely surprised as to how they attracted such a cruel fate. Yet the harm they do to others releases malevolence that usually eventually contaminates them as well.

By the way, Roberto, I know I have thanked you before, but I want to thank you again in these pages for the world to read, for being in my life when I most needed it. I miss your silly jokes, how you always teased me and just for being delightfully goofy. I am writing this here because I will make sure you get a copy of my book, and hope you still – and always -feel as special as you made me feel.

Fifteen years after Roberto, when living in Chicago again, I would meet Adam who has somehow – miraculously, it seems - helped me believe again, that two people can be good to each other, respect each other - and to finally love again. I hit the jackpot, as they say, with him. He really loves me for who I am, no questions asked.

"Every moment of your life is infinitely creative and the universe is endlessly bountiful. Just put forth a clear enough request, and everything your heart truly desires must come to you. **Shakti Gawain.**

CHAPTER 8

❦

WHEN I WAS 37, RAFY and I moved to Florida from Puerto Rico. As described before, that ended terribly, and was followed by a lot of soul-searching, and the wonderful time with Roberto.

But after the store Roberto and I started failed and he went back to Italy, I again needed to work. But I couldn't find a job cutting hair, because the salons in South Florida were rigid about each stylist having a hair license. So in 1999, I went to a privately funded charitable vocational institution that would help people who wanted to go to school by paying for their education. It was a three month application process; eventually I got accepted, and went to Pivot Point La Belle Beauty Academy in Miami.

At first, I started to do the same thing at Pivot Point as I did at my previous schools, all the way back to childhood. I let my mind wander during any training that didn't include actually working with my hands. But the Pivot Point people were very strict, and I saw that this time, I truly needed to take the book learning part of the education seriously. So I started going to class pretty consistently, and only missed a few days.

But at this time, once again, I didn't have a place to live, because the friend I had been living with began to drink heavily. I would no longer tolerate such an environment, and packed up and walked out. As a result, I was sleeping where I could, and keeping clean by using South Beach public showers, which are located right on the sidewalks. And when I was at school, I would shave in their bathrooms, and otherwise clean myself up.

I should point out that by this time, my own use of recreational drugs and alcohol had dropped off considerably. Having been an aggressive party boy for so long, the crazed pursuit of pleasure no longer possessed me.

I lived this way for about the first month of school. Eventually, I saved enough money to move to a hotel with a friend, but he soon disappeared, and I couldn't pay the rent and also buy food. I managed to stay in this hotel but it was totally overrun with roaches and mice, and had nothing but bums and drug addicts as tenants. During this period, for breakfast I would eat a piece of chocolate, and for dinner, a bowl of rice; this went on for about two months, while I was in school. This wasn't really enough food to sustain a healthy adult, but I had to choose between rent and food, and didn't want to be back on the street, even in sunny Florida.

I applied for food stamps and also started to make money on the Pivot Point's training floor, doing clients' hair. I was already very good at it, so the clients would tip me very well, and I started saving that money, and my Supplemental Security Insurance (SSI) checks (which I had been getting since I was about 29). Doing that enabled me to move into a studio apartment right next door to the beauty school and away from the beach, and its many distractions and temptations.

In my studio, I had very few possessions; a TV, a blow-up mattress, a set of weights, a few dishes and a bike - all I needed at the time. I left home each weekday morning and went to school every day from 9 a.m. to 9 p.m. I would stay there and just kept learning, absorbing everything I could from the instructors and students, while becoming very popular in school.

Everyone there loved me, especially the girls; I would do their hair and in return (since they knew about my money situation), they would buy me lunch, or groceries or just bring enough lunch to share with me. My training at Pivot Point was a very touching and special time in my life, and I met many wonderful people from all over the world.

The school course lasted around ten months to a year, but being in a hurry, I finished it all in eight months, compressing my hours. Most important for my academic success though, I got creative with my class notes and textbooks. I started to color highlight whatever was really important for me to know, and let me tell you, those pages looked like a rainbow.

As I've explained, my early education had been very poor. I didn't really learn to read in school, only very gradually picked it up in my teens and twenties when it was necessary for adult activities. I had never gotten really good at it, or at writing (in either English or Spanish). Thus, learning by reading alone was still very hard for me, so the "color codes" I added to customize my course books were very helpful, a more visual method of learning.

During this period, I carried my notes and books with me everywhere I went, and studied everything, by colors, over and over until it was engraved on my brain. Even if I already knew the answers to whatever process was being described, I would still study my material again. I would go to a park nearby in Coconut Grove, and work out on the exercise bars and tan, studying between sets. If I was on a city bus or train or on the beach, I would carry my notes with me, studying them like my Bible.

While I was in school, I would study with all the students, and ask a lot of questions of my instructors. They were all very impressed with me, and frankly, I was impressed with myself, amazed at what I was achieving. This gave me a sense of accomplishment that was an unfamiliar for me, and it felt wonderful – in some ways, better than any recreational drug. And since I was studying something I truly liked and excelled at, it was especially satisfying.

Finally, I finished school, completing the Florida licenses required, 1200 hours; my grades were all A's, and B's (and a single D, which I turned into a B), well ahead of schedule. Then I passed my school test which (as it turned out) was actually harder than the state's Beautician Licensing board test.

I passed the school's final exam with a score of 80, which was a B (if I hadn't raced through the course faster than normal, my score would surely have been higher). My date to take the Florida state board Beautician's license test was a month later, and until then, I did nothing but study at home or anywhere I was.

Finally, the day for my test arrived, and I will never forget it. Visiting Miami Beach the day before, I told, my few remaining friends that the reason they hadn't seen me in months was because I'd been in beauty school. In the party atmosphere of South Florida, it is common for acquaintances to drop out of sight like that – no one gets alarmed by it. They wanted to celebrate with me, and got me so drunk that when I got up the next morning -- the day of the test --I was ghastly sick. I had to take two buses to get to the test site, and it was so hot I was sweating like crazy and while on the bus, I wanted to throw up. But finally, damp and woozy, I got to my destination.

I was sent into a dark room full of computers, on one of which I had to answer around 120 questions. They gave us a time frame of about an hour to finish, but I ripped through that hugely complex test in about 25 minutes, then told the officials there that I was done. They were amazed at my speed. "What? You're done?!"

"Yes, I am."

They checked my test immediately, and I had passed with a grade of 90 percent! I was so shocked I wanted to cry from excitement! I went over to my school that same day to share my marvelous news with everyone there, and when I showed them my grade, they were nearly as surprised and thrilled as I was! You see, most people have to take the Florida state board test at least two or three times to pass it, because it is so hard, but (for me at least), it was actually easier than the Pivot Point final I'd taken a month earlier.

For somebody who had never in his life really achieved much of anything – whose life up to this point had basically been a struggle to survive, alternating with frenetic efforts to blot out that reality with drugs, etc. – success like this was intoxicating. I had actually, really *done* something! As satisfying as my sense of achievement at my diligent studying had been, the thrill of triumph at sailing through this ferocious test – while hung over yet! – was nearly indescribable.

That same day, the owner of my school, Pivot Point asked me to come into her office to congratulate me, and she handed me a refund check for more than $800, because I had finished school in eight months, which was way ahead of schedule. Then she asked me if I would like to become a teacher in her school. I was so surprised and felt so special; to teach at a Pivot Point school, one really has to be great at hair care, so it was really a huge compliment to me.

But marvelous as the offer was, I didn't accept. Instead, I immediately started working at a salon and moved back near Miami's beachfront. It was a truly great achievement for me to finally have my license and to actually look at it in my hands! After so many years of trying, this definitively showed me that when a person wants something badly enough, things that had seemed impossible come within reach.

I graduated from Pivot Point in the summer of 2001, with bright prospects for a career doing work I loved and performed superbly. I began working Saturdays at a salon I'd started at while finishing my training, but once again – just as HIV had infected me – an event of worldwide significance impacted me personally: The attacks of September 11 of that year.

At the time, the American economy had already been weakening due to the bursting of the "Internet Startup Bubble," but then the fear sown by the attacks sent it into a tailspin. A great deal of leisure spending stopped, and business plummeted at the salon where I was working.

After that, I couldn't earn enough money to pay for necessities, so my fine new qualifications and I were adrift again. Worse, because I was HIV+, it was vital that I retain my Social Security benefits to pay for my life-saving medications. And as it happened, at about this time, one of my many ex-lovers from Chicago, Bob, was visiting South Beach for a party. Hearing of my difficult situation, he invited me to drive back north with him and stay at his place while trying to make a life there again.

I knew that I would have trouble finding work in Chicago too, but still had family there, the aunts and cousins I'd lived with during adolescence. Further, it was easier in Illinois than in Florida to get the social benefits I would need to survive until my hair care practice could take root. So I accepted Bob's offer, packed a single suitcase, gave away or abandoned my other meager possessions and rode back to Chicago with him.

I didn't want to return to a cold climate, but in late 2001, there was real fear that society might break down if there were another terrorist attack.

As terrible as my life with my father had been, my extended family back in Chicago were fine people, and would have given me refuge, had it been necessary. I had no such support in South Florida; my bar buddies there might party with me, but would not have actually kept me alive.

As I have, and will, throughout this book, I will take this occasion to express gratitude and admiration for people I have never previously thanked properly. I dearly love my family in Chicago – my aunts and cousins – who, as an adult, I now realize to be truly wonderful. I am proud to be related to those people who helped and accepted me without judging.

So, my dear and loving family (who, if they read this book, may be learning for the first time what my life was like when I was back in Puerto Rico and Florida), thank you so much for being there for me in the early 2000s, and even more so when I was in my teens. Back then, I didn't realize how precious it was to have a stable, caring family to rely on. Most young people don't, but this is especially true for one who had been surrounded by irresponsible, live-for-the-moment adults as I had been – and who was also blinded by his own pain.

I cannot name you all here, but if you helped and protected me when it was most needed, you know who you are. You are finally getting the story of how I survived and developed after I left your care and protection. And to any of my loving relations who have already passed away, I offer my special thanks, and my hopes for your happiness wherever you are, and in your next lives.

Speaking of gratitude, let me describe some relevant background of my emotional development. As adult readers will know, when we are children, most of us are not terribly aware of, or sensitive to, the rights, needs and feelings of those around us. Such concern for others is "empathy," and learning it is a major part of the normal, healthy process of maturing. But because my early life was so different from most people (abused in every possible sense), this part of the growth process played out differently for me, and would only come much later in life.

When I was young, I had no one to advise me about proper emotional development. My father, a brutish, ignorant and selfish man, couldn't have done it even if he'd cared, nor could most of the dysfunctional (like Delores) people he brought into my life. Besides that, I had experienced far too little of the generosity that empathy needs to take root. I usually didn't have or feel real security, and there were many times when my very survival really was at risk. In such situations, people will focus exclusively on their own needs – especially if they are young children who know no better. Such was my case.

And by the time I was living with my extended family in Chicago with the toxic tempest of being with my father, I had no experience of trust. My family in Chicago thoroughly deserved my trust, but at the time I couldn't even realize that, let alone grant it to them.

In fact, I avoided bonding emotionally with them or anyone else at the time, because so many people in my life – my abuela, Estelle, friends in the Bronx, my cousins in Puerto Rico – had been taken from me by death or by my father's disregard of my well-being, that I became defensive and didn't become close to anyone. I didn't do this consciously, it was just a primitive survival instinct.

In fact, I'm not sure what I had with Eddy, Rafy, or any lovers up to Roberto, involved actual "bonding." What we had may have been codependence, or sexual gratification – but not bonding, in which a connection of mutual care develops between two people.

Setting down my life story forces me to reflect on what events and experiences made me the person I now am. My terrible childhood could easily have led me to the gutter and an early grave, yet it did not. So this book is not only the tale of how I tried to find hope in a life with precious little reason for me to feel any, but of how that process is ongoing, even as I write.

To continue with the story of my return to Chicago late in 2001, I stayed at Bob's place for only a few weeks. I badly wanted a home of my own, but couldn't earn enough money to rent one because, as expected, the hairstyling business was greatly reduced by the economic crisis at the time; and in any case, to be hired by a local salon I would need to get an Illinois beautician's licence.

My modest SSI funds were enough for me to get a small apartment in a shabby corner of Chicago's Uptown neighborhood. It wasn't much, but I dearly wanted my privacy, so was glad not to need a roommate. And for the next few months of 2001 and into 2002, at age 40, I reverted to the life I'd had in my twenties, binging on drinks, drugs and sex. After my diligence in getting my Pivot Point degree and Florida license, after losing Roberto and being mistreated by Rafy, and after moving from sunny South Beach to chilly Chicago, my instinct (or whatever reasons) was to lose myself in unattached fun for a while.

Money was still a major problem for me at the time, but some salons would overlook my Florida beautician's license. They could not hire me outright, but some of them would call me to work when they were short-handed.

An incident at this time very nearly cost me my life. One day, I came into a salon hoping for a walk-in client, and the owner told me that he already had one waiting, and warned me that this would be a real challenge.

Readers who know of the mythological "Gorgon," Medusa, will have some idea of the sight that confronted me. Whether this woman, a

Latina, had been confined somewhere and unable to reach a hairdresser, or simply had a bizarre sense of fashion, I never learned, but she had the biggest load of head hair I had ever seen. It was very dense like a lion's mane, yet also seemed to writhe like Medusa's snakes. None of the other stylists were free, so they told me to try to tame the follicular monster.

This lady's horrifying hair didn't turn me into stone, but it did – literally – give me a heart attack; I do not exaggerate; the shock of this person's appearance and the realization that I was expected to subdue it caused a shock of pain in my chest, followed by aching in my arms, shortness of breath, and nausea.

I was obviously seriously ill, but we all just assumed it was a panic attack. A friend came and took me to a nearby hospital, where they stabilized me, and after some tests, informed me that I had suffered a mild heart attack!

I was a slender man who exercised a lot, even when I couldn't afford a gym, so I didn't fit the image of the typical person with cardiac problems. But the doctors, after inquiring into my lifestyle, explained that my appearance was offset by my very unhealthy diet, heavy drinking and drug use, and the fact that I had an undiagnosed heart murmur. And of course, though it hadn't registered with me up to that point, I was now middle-aged.

In terms of health, I'd had one immense stroke of good luck: I never became sick due to my HIV status, and now attribute this to my denial. At the time, I simply refused to accept that I might get sick – and did not. Denial had been another of my defense mechanisms for dealing with many of the worst problems and experiences in my life. I would suppress my memories, pretend things hadn't happened, downplay their importance – anything but confront them in all their true ghastliness. This had become a lifelong pattern for me – a survival reaction.

And so, denial was my response to being told I'd had a heart attack. While still in the hospital, at one point, I started to exercise in my bed, doing sit-ups and pushups, but was still attached to various monitors, and my elevated heart activity brought a team of emergency staff running to my room. Needless to say, when they saw that my heart activity had suddenly spiked because of my calisthenics, they got upset, and instantly ordered me to stop.

They told me that, in addition to scaring them and forcing wasteful use of vital hospital resources, it was clear I wasn't taking my situation as seriously as necessary. My very life was in danger but I was still focused on looking attractive. The medical people told me that in addition to my heart murmur, I had other anatomical problems, aggravated by my HIV medications. So if I hoped to stay alive, I needed to change my priorities: My actual health, not just my appearance, absolutely had to take precedence. Also, they sedated me for the rest of my time there, to prevent anymore over-exertion.

And my refraining from stressful exercise was not the only change of lifestyle they demanded: they said I had to halt my use of recreational drugs, severely restrict my use of alcohol and tobacco, and worst of all, stop eating many of the things I most enjoyed. Despite my being slender, food had been one of my most reliable comforts in life. In particular, I loved cheese, and it was one of the things I was explicitly told not to eat anymore.

All of this was too much of a shock for me. It would have been hard for any previously healthy person to accept such news. But since adolescence, I'd learned to live for the moment, and suddenly being told that my life depended on breaking old habits and depriving myself of pleasures I took for granted, was a probably a far higher level of difficulty greater for me than for most people, and it demanded a seismic shift of my mindset. My whole relationship to life had to change, if life itself was to be preserved.

I wasn't even able to grasp the need for such a change yet, let alone to actually make it. At this point, early in 2002, I was still fairly new to Chicago, and during my stay in the hospital, only one person visited me. None of the urgent information the medical staff told me registered with me. With my habit of filtering out bad news it was as if the medical people were talking to someone else, and I was just a witness who could safely ignore their instructions.

Thus, when I was discharged from the hospital (with a bagful of new medications and strict orders about diet and permissible activities), I was given money for cab fare so I wouldn't have the stress of walking to my home, about two miles distant. I got into the cab, but as soon as we were out of sight of the hospital, told the driver to let me out, and proceeded to walk home, to regain the muscle tone lost during my confinement to bed.

My tiny apartment's two windows faced brick walls, so it was always dark there. Ever since I had been raped by my uncle in a dark room, any lack of light has severely affected my mood, but this time, the darkness – somehow - enlightened me. That depressing space brought home to me – finally – that I had just nearly died of a heart attack! Once I absorbed that, it became vital for me to move someplace with more light, and at least some view other than bricks. I knew my mood, in that dim room, would be a constant threat to my health.

So I found a small, but clean and safe apartment in Chicago's East Lakeview neighborhood, also called "Boystown," and the heart of the city's gay community. It was a more expensive area to live in than Uptown, but acquaintances were always paying to take me out drinking, dining, etc. My personality was still attracting that kind of positivity.

It was around this time that I received another marvelous act of kindness from a local relative. My cousin Wilbur, knowing that I couldn't be hired in a Chicago salon until I got an Illinois beautician's license, paid me one thousand dollars for a single haircut. He didn't tell me he was going to, just came by my place for a styling, then departed, telling me my payment was in an envelope he'd left with me. When I opened it, there was $1,000 cash in it Wilbur was not rich, so his generosity was all the more remarkable, and enabled me to pay for the training I needed for an Illinois license, which I immediately got at a local school. Needless to say, I will always cut Wilbur's hair for free anytime he wants.

I now sometimes wonder if such exceptional, and to me especially, unfamiliar acts of kindness were not starting to work on my subconscious mind then, hinting to me that life could be genuinely good – not just a cycle of misery alternating with sensual excess to blot out the terrible realities.

But beyond moving to more cheerful surroundings that improved my mood and health, I ignored the rest of the medical recommendations that had been provided, still eating what I liked and using drugs and alcohol with virtually no restraint. In retrospect, it's surprising I have survived to write this.

My carelessness was not entirely a lack of understanding of the graveness of my situation, nor even to denial alone. At this point, I still did not realize how unusually dreadful my life had been compared to most people, let alone understand how it had warped my view of life. After all, I had no other experience to compare mine to, so didn't realize all the ways it was harming me. Denial was my main strategy for coping and surviving, so I had begun to use it automatically (but not consciously) in most difficult situations. Another result of my early life was, as noted, never to "bond" with other people, or try to see events from any perspective (or advantage) but my own.

But the limitations of denial's usefulness – like not following medical advice after a heart attack – could not be ignored forever. Eventually, I would be forced to confront the very things I had been trying to wish away. Events to be described later in this book led me – finally – to seek professional emotional counseling.

I was now 41 years old, and no longer a kid – even though I still felt in just about every respect like I was a teenager or a young guy in my 20s at most. Maybe it was a result of having my childhood stolen from me. Nonetheless, I was at a crossroads. I could choose to nurse the bitterness of my past, and lash out at life and at other people - or use my talents and the sunny disposition I'd been born with (which had nearly been smothered by the ordeals of my life) to make the world around me as close to heaven as possible.

The more light you allow within you, the brighter the world you live in will be. Shakti Gawain

CHAPTER 9

❧

AFTER I HAD LIVED IN the East Lakeview apartment for about two years, a friend who worked for the state of Illinois told me about a subsidized apartment that was available back in my old Uptown neighborhood. I liked where I was living, but the place being offered cost less than half my current rent, had a reasonable amount of space, was fairly clean, seemed safe, and had adequate basic amenities. So I accepted my friend's help, and moved to that subsidized building.

One of the main reasons I wanted inexpensive housing was that by that time I was developing incipient arthritis in my hands from the stress of years of cutting hair. I could no longer do unlimited amounts of such work, even if it had been readily available (which it still wasn't). So getting this apartment would free much of my modest income for other enterprises, including several small inventions of my own which I wanted to develop and market for the beauty and luxury industries. Also, by this time my spending for alcohol and recreational drugs had plunged. I still socialized a lot, and if someone offered to treat me to such things now, I'd accept, but having done so much of that when I was younger, it was no longer a priority for me.

I worked on those inventions and other proposed enterprises because I truly disliked taking public money in the form of SSI. One of the few positive things that must be said for my father was that he always worked. He didn't expect the government (or any of his women) to support him. And I felt the same; I wanted to work, but the job I was truly good at (and really liked) – beauty work – is inherently unstable, one of the first things most consumers will cut back if times get hard. Besides, as noted, hair care's physical toll had begun to tell on me. So I returned to Uptown, and that inexpensive apartment.

The consequences of my heart attack had not vanished, but they didn't preoccupy me. As I'd hoped, moving from my previous dark apartment in Uptown to the sunny one in Lakeview had immensely helped my mood. And my new, subsidized flat also had lots of natural light, but came with a cost not measured in money. Outside my front door was the most depressing environment I had lived in for many years. My new neighbors were the kind of people I'd seen as a child in the ghastly South Bronx, with major drug addictions, alcoholism, serious criminal histories – people who really had no other place to live. In fact, the top two floors of my building were exclusively for people recovering from chemical dependence.

My health got better, but my mood got worse, as I began to be impacted by these surroundings. Instead of improving my life, it felt like I was falling backward. However, I would observe the semi-ruined souls in my area, and wonder how I had not ended up as they had, my life wrecked by addictions and irresponsible choices. Certainly, there had been many of both in my past, but the difference was that, although I enjoyed them at the time, they never seized control of me. Somehow, the abyss of crime and poverty which I had feared had not snared me.

But a different chasm, that of emotional desolation, now yawned before me. My desire to pull my own weight seemed to make me different from many of the people in my new building, who truly didn't seem to want to work (or had made mistakes that made them unemployable). That wasn't my attitude at all – it never was. I wanted to work, to support myself, and even to become affluent.

But I hadn't avoided that new chasm yet. My distress at my apparent inability to move, once and for all, away from poverty and turbulence continued to grow. Then I learned I was eligible for psychological counseling at virtually no cost through the same gay social service agency that had arranged my HIV medications.

Given everything that had happened to me in my life up to this point, I probably needed counseling as badly as anyone, but quite simply didn't realize it. Turmoil, instability and mistreatment were "normal" for me, and it had never occurred to me that they might have made me fundamentally different from most people. Nor had it occurred to me that my difficult birth, childhood and adolescence need not keep me from happiness forever.

And frankly, being 44 years old by this time, I was also alarmed at seeing the first inescapable signs of aging in my appearance: hair loss, wrinkling skin, and of most concern, that incipient arthritis in my hands. No one likes being forced to see such signs of mortality, and realizing that my youth was passing deepened my sorrow that I had experienced so little of youth's supposed sweetness.

So when this latest unhappiness (at my return to squalor) coincided with easy access to counseling, I decided to take advantage of it, and was assigned to a counselor recommended by the clinic, a woman named Laura.

I went to talk to her about my confusion at my current living situation, and how, to me, it felt like backsliding. In an effort to understand why I felt so strongly about my current home and life, she asked me probing questions about my personal history. As I've explained, I'd long been in denial about the depth of the most traumatic experiences of my life. Not denial in the sense that I pretended I hadn't been abandoned, raped or beaten, but denial that such experiences were especially awful.

As I told Laura all of this over the course of several sessions, looks of deepening horror visibly came over her face - followed by silent tears. Gradually, she made clear to me that my life story was one of the most tragic she had ever heard – and working in this part of Chicago, she had heard some pretty horrifying ones. She was the first person to use the term "denial" to me, to explain how I was deliberately (though only semi-consciously so) downplaying the scars with which life had marked me.

But she also told me it was amazing that I had turned out to be relatively productive, and to be an overall asset to society. Many people with burdens like mine are simply crushed by them, and lose the ability to function as independent adults. So in that sense, "denial" had actually been good for me; it had enabled me to survive to a point in life when I might be able to withstand the truth – and even to vanquish any harm it might still have the power do to me.

Working with her, I discovered that I had, in fact, actually long suspected that my life was far worse than that of most other people. It had so much misfortune in it that it probably seemed like a Puerto Rican parody of a Charles Dickens story, with some ghastly ill-starred central character. But to keep from being overwhelmed by a sense of personal tragedy, I'd had to pretend the horror wasn't as intense as it was.

And I was to learn that this halted emotional development still left me a shot at staying "young at heart" – a more important, and authentic, attribute of youth than smooth skin and thick hair.

This woman had forced me to confront the awful truths about my life (at the same time I had to face getting older), but doing so was my first step to actual healing. She pointed out that my life was a set of ruins, but that she could begin helping me clear them out so as to leave a new foundation on which to build happiness. Not pleasure, not immediate gratification, but true contentment - a concept so seemingly out of reach I never even dared think it was possible until Laura told me that it was on my horizon, and she could help me reach it.

And without specifically intending to, she was preparing me for love. After my nightmarish affair and breakup with Rafy in my mid-30s, I had decided to never fall deeply in love again. Roberto was very dear to me, and we enjoyed each other immensely, but no potential emotional reward seemed worth the risk of repeating the agonizing self-inflicted wound of Rafy again, so I did "love" Robert but I couldn't fall in love.

But my counselor enabled me to start to see that I had been trying to find, in a relationship with another man, the affection and acceptance that had been denied me in childhood, when they were most needed. And when that unsatisfied hunger got blended with lustful physical attraction (as to Rafy, and to a lesser extent, many others), the result was a poisonous potion of emotional hemlock, which seemed to addict me as surely as any narcotic deliberately taken for thrills.

She helped me recognize my repeated cycle of seeking validation where it was not to be found, and to break it - without feeling that my only option was to spurn love entirely. Indeed, I think it's probably fair to say that most people had not earned as much right to taste the true sweetness of life as I had, after having nearly drowned in so many forms of its bitterness.

Laura explained to me that the constant fear I felt as a result of all the terrible things that had happened to me was still affecting me, warping my judgment and perceptions. She told me to be conscious of when my fear reflex was grabbing hold of me, then to, "Treat it like a baby; speaking soothingly to my fear/baby, but then leave it in its crib and walk away from it."

It occurs to me that this was remarkably similar to what my mother had done to me after I was born; abandoned me in a hammock. Laura surely didn't intend it that way, but to me, the similarity was unmistakable.

She also recognized that I had Attention Deficit Disorder (ADD), which was the reason I found it so difficult to learn and focus. She gave me a strategy of "changing channels" (as with an old television with dials); if my life was on a channel that was upsetting me, I was simply to mentally change it to one I liked.

Gradually, Laura's suggestions and insights began to take hold, and my whole life became more stable, practically and emotionally. I left my fear in the crib, and started working on the raft of inventions I had long had at the back of my mind.

I had always been, generally, a happy person (despite my constant fear), but with Laura's advice, this outlook became more noticeable.

People around me in the squalid apartment building noticed this change, and began asking me how I could be so upbeat given that I was living in such a place. I was surprised by their questions, not aware of how apparent the change in me was. So Laura's input truly helped to transform my whole life.

While all this emotional reconstruction was happening, I was also starting to achieve my purpose for having moved to the apartment in Uptown: I was saving a good deal of money. As I said, it was starting to hurt my hands to cut hair, so I was using the saved funds to try to promote inventions I had conceived.

Over the several years I lived in that tumultuous (but cheap) building, I managed to save several thousand dollars. This money went to develop products such as a salon glove (to protect a stylist from getting cut during hair cutting), a mist-spray bottle for warm water (during hairdressing), a pillow hoody (for darkness during sleep), a special mat to scour the feet during a shower, sunglasses with head hugging clips to hold them in place during active movement (like jogging) - etc. I obtained short term, provisional patents for each of these.

I'm currently working on my own product called H. Abreu's Vitamin Hair Gel, and my app, "one dollar hairstylist" with which I teach people to do their hair at home very inexpensively and at onedollarhairstylist. com. I am still working on these two endeavors, hopefully witch I will see flourish in this life time and this book your reading as well, witch am very proud of. My other endeavors have proved to be financially viable. I sent presentations about each of them to dozens of manufacturers and distributors - few of whom even bothered to respond.

However, that is not really the point: The real lesson was that, by this time, I had learned to let nothing - nothing - crush my spirit. When one project (hope) failed, I just went on to the next one - because believe me, I've learned that life is always presenting us with reasons to hope. And hope is invariably the better option than despair.

During my deeply painful struggles with the newly-recognized tragedy of my life, I was still pushing ahead on another major front.

Some months after I stopped seeing Laura, and while I was still following her advice with regards to fearlessly pursuing my inventions, life offered me the chance to apply her wisdom on an entirely different front: I met a lovely man, named Adam.

"You create your opportunities by asking for them."

Shakti Gawain

CHAPTER 10

❦

Adam and I met in 2008 via a gay online dating site, and our attraction to each other was strong from the first. But whereas Adam immediately saw me as someone he could love, for me the attraction was exclusively – and deliberately – physical. As I've said before, after my long series of unsatisfying quasi "relationships" – the last, with Rafy, being the most agonizing – I had decided I was through with love. I never sought, nor wanted, a romantic connection again, even though other men had often wanted to have them with me.

But the way we related to each other was different from the start. Not only was he smarter and more responsible than most of the other men I had dated, but he was the first one who seemed able to actually see beyond the surface I presented to the world. He saw beyond the vulnerability behind that, to a deeper level of myself, a level whose existence even I wasn't fully aware of. Rather like hearing one's own voice for the first time on a recording, we very often cannot see how we appear to others, especially if the other is as sensitive and perceptive as Adam. He saw things in me that I only suspected were there.

But at first, I wanted to follow the pattern that had served me well since Rafy. Adam and I could date, have intimacy, travel together, etc. I was willing to share anything but romance. At first Adam pretended to agree to that. But later, after we had become a couple, he confessed that he never really accepted my restrictions. He had known all along that if he gave me all that he had to offer, eventually, my "moat" of self-protection would evaporate, and he would be able to finally pierce the shield I had built around my heart.

And he was right.

When we met, I was still living in my subsidized apartment, which I had made an oasis of calm, color and delight in a building housing dozens of shattered lives. Adam lived just a few blocks away in a space far larger than mine, but gradually he spent more and more time at my place, spending almost every night with me.

He had a sharp, efficient intelligence, very different from my more artistic sensibilities, and had had high-paying jobs before, earning far more than I ever had. By the time we met, he was managing a fairly high-end furniture and decorative accessories store, work at which he excelled.

I was still struggling financially, living only on my S.S.I. income. By this time, it was clear that as much as I loved beauty work, it was never going to make me rich, so my main hope for financial security rested with the many personal care inventions my imagination kept churning out. And since my housing was so inexpensive, a lot of my modest income was going into my inventions, refining their design, producing marketing materials, contacting manufacturers and retailers, etc.

And Adam showed his willingness to share my life by gamely pitching into these enterprises. As of this writing, no substantial return has come from any of them. But it was a sign of true partnership that he would cast his lot with me to help me try to make my dreams – not just of inventions, but of the prosperity that might have come from them – realities.

After we had been dating more than two years, Adam was virtually living with me in my tiny apartment, using his own place mostly to store his wardrobe, and space for occasional privacy. But my neighbors still made me uncomfortable, and I began to feel that moving to Adam's home as he had long suggested, aside from its being far larger, offered me a final escape from life at the margins of society, a life I had struggled for many years to evade. A true separation seemed impossible if I continued to live under the same roof as recovering alcoholics, drug addicts, and people with criminal backgrounds.

I did not judge my neighbors; from my own background, I know how very well how people's lives can be altered by circumstances they did not ask for, and cannot control. But I had fought long and fiercely to lift myself out of that trap and my efforts to do so were still inconclusive and precarious. Adam had come from a stable middle class Puerto Rican background, the very opposite of mine. His life was prosperous and orderly, and joining his environment offered me hope to draw a line, once and for all, between me and a life that had long been little more than a daily fight for survival.

Besides, by this time Adam had given me much reason to believe he could be trusted with my heart. But before agreeing to move into his apartment, I made some very candid ground rules: I could live with him, but he could not expect me to actually love him, and to keep intimacy exclusively for him. But in addition to respecting my comfort zone, Adam did not see this – a so-called "open relationship" – as necessarily a bad thing.

Complete monogamy is a beautiful ideal, and the stuff of romantic legend, but pursuing it as the only acceptable goal can "make the perfect the enemy of the good." There are many drawbacks to being a gay man, but one advantage can be (though not always) that both parties to a sexual encounter, or even a relationship are "playing from the same book." Generally speaking, males and females have different sexual needs, preferences, and mechanics, which have led to ages of conflict and problems between the sexes. But two men can more easily agree, if they will, to keep "sex" and "love" separate.

So Adam and I agreed to have a relationship in which both of us were free to pursue sexual activities without the other, or by bringing others temporarily into our union. This was very different from the conventional ideal, but for us, it not only worked for a long time, but kept our own relationship vigorous and growing.

For after I moved to Adam's apartment, I was around him constantly and away from my own cramped space and the tense, sad atmosphere of my former apartment building. My defenses began to soften, and love – true love – with this kind and beautiful man gradually began to seem like the next logical step.

So I fell in love with Adam, and we became partners in every sense. As trust grew, he came to mean to me all the things that the men I'd been involved with before should have meant – but did not. That is, Adam showed me the joy of giving of myself for love by the example of how he gave to me. This was a revelation to me, as my previous relationships had been largely either about taking from the other person, or about giving in unhealthy, needy, desperate-for-affection patterns.

Being with Adam seemed to open me to learn the "right" way to love, a mature, selfless, life-affirming way. What I had learned from my counselor about how I'd been in denial about all the emotional and physical violence that had been done to me began to play out in practical form now. I wanted Adam, rather than needed him. And from that willingness to let our lives intertwine like the roots and branches of adjacent trees, I was able to develop a union with Adam immeasurably deeper than any of the survival-instinct, immediate gratification-oriented ones in my past.

We were content sharing our lives in his spacious apartment for more than a year. But it was a basement unit, and though we did our best to make it cheerful, even elegant, I still needed sunlight to thrive, and natural illumination could not reach this space.

So in November of 2011, we found an apartment back in Chicago's main gay neighborhood, Lakeview. It was a large "loft" studio, but had an excellent location and lots of the nourishing sunlight my spirit craved.

Thus, Adam and I moved into the first home we had chosen together, and the first home I had picked with a partner since my catastrophic move to the Miami apartment with Rafy many years earlier. My hopes were high as I was finally living in a nice (if not luxurious) space with someone I cared about. Moreover, Adam, with his larger, more reliable income, generously continued to help me fund my beauty product inventions, and paid most of the rent, while I used my public aid to buy our groceries and cover smaller household expenses.

I was very happy in our studio, but Adam wanted more space, and later, when a larger, duplex apartment became available in our building, he did his best to get me to move there. Content with our current space, I resisted at first, but since he clearly wanted the larger unit so badly – and since he had accommodated me so often – I relented for the sake of his happiness, and we moved to the larger apartment.

It faced west, and soaked up sunlight much of the time, a radiance that reflected the happiness that grew in me there. After all my suffering, all my counseling, self-examination and Buddhist meditation, the fabric of my life, which Fate had frayed so often and so callously, seemed to be coming together. Contentment in work, love and life seemed to be within sight at last.

That was not an illusion, but it was not to be a permanent reality. Factors in Adam's life, and in our relationship, that had long smoldered suddenly burst into destroying flame, burning up my hopes with it – again.

On June 15, 2013 – seven days before our four-year anniversary - Adam's commitment to me froze and died. He ejected me from his heart, literally from one day to the next. On June 14, he had called or texted me several times to say he loved me, had kissed me all over – just as he'd done for the previous four years.

And then the idyll and my fond hopes were over. It felt as if I blinked and the entire world had changed when my eyes reopened, for my world had indeed changed. Not only did Adam suddenly tell me that he was desperately unhappy and unsatisfied in our relationship, but he did so with words and actions that he deliberately chose to hurt me. It was surreal that this sweet, adoring man could abruptly become so angry and cruel, saying things to me, whom he had surely loved and whose terrible youth he knew all about, that I would never imagine he could say to anyone. The change happened so swiftly that it was as if he had been hijacked by a demon.

Adam told me he'd been seeing a therapist who had identified various things that were wrong with our relationship, but I suspect this was only a cover story. I believe that his decision to leap out of love was because he had started an affair with another man, since a new lover was suddenly in his life very shortly after June 15 – too soon, it seemed, for it to have started after we had split. He may have felt that it would have been too hurtful to me to reveal this, or that it reflected badly on him.

But in fact, maintaining this tale harmed us both, for it damaged him beyond recognition. He changed unrecognizably the day he left me, corrupting from being sweet, kind, and loving to a crude iceman, not merely indifferent to, but contemptuous of the feelings, of another person. I also suspect that he may have been using drugs in the time leading to the breakup, which literally distorted his memory and judgment, causing him to make false assertions that I had manipulated and used him.

Another sad aspect of all this is that, whatever the true sources of his dissatisfaction with me (if any), we could have resolved them if he'd only told me about them so we could discuss them. But Adam, though a very open and transparent person in many ways, had always kept certain feelings entirely to himself, so that even as well as I knew him, his inmost thoughts were unknown to me. So aside from the ferocity of his attack, I was shattered by its ambush quality, having believed that my relationship with Adam was perfectly solid. Then I was left wondering if it could have been prevented, if only he'd communicated it to me.

All this is doubly sad because, as of this writing, Adam does not, cannot, see it this way - being so blinded, confused and deep in pain - that he's hiding behind the madness of the frigid new personality he has adopted.

Even more bewildering, after his heartless words and deeds, he would later blame me for all the pain the breakup caused him. I am not unbiased, but there is no way such an accusation could make sense to me, so (having known him intimately for four years), I am pretty sure that he has simply projected shame at his own behavior onto me. That is, he felt terrible because he knew he had done wrong, but was blaming me in order to deflect his own feelings of guilt.

Adam made me feel like no one else has in all my relationships, so therefore to me, this was really like my first true, authentic, mature love. Such a disappointment – especially, since I had never intended to become emotionally involved again with another person – was as stunning as being abruptly thrust into airless outer space must be.

But unlike the way my life and sanity began to unravel after my affair with Rafy failed, my breakup with Adam only deeply saddened me. I did not unconsciously seek "validation" in loving Adam– or him loving me – as I had sought in earlier romances, an emotional hunger that repelled various lovers before.

Although there may still have been some element of that between Adam and me, I know it wasn't the main reason our relationship came to an end; it did so mainly because of some dissatisfaction on his part, more than mine. Given the sort of life we had been creating together, that seems uniquely sad. I shall miss him, but can and will learn from this ordeal, then move forward with my life. Of all the sad things about this story, the saddest may be that, whatever plans Adam I had for life after me seem to have failed, and, as of this writing, he is miserably regretful for ending our relationship at all, let alone as cruelly as he did.

But it has led to a leap forward for me – although an agonizing one, like leaping over a cauldron of flames. For my life is now about far more than whom I love, and who loves me. I'm deeply hurt, have a great void inside me, but now have faith that it will heal. It's already doing so every day more and more. It's going to be okay – I will be okay.

After the rupture with Adam, I responded as I always had before to failed relationships; with an outburst of overindulgence in sex, drugs and liquor – any stimulation to numb the heartache.

Yet I had grown emotionally since my previous breakup in ways that hadn't been apparent before. At one time, such an orgy, and the sorrow it was meant to soothe, would have lasted for a whole year, but this time, after only ten days or so, I consciously decided that this was pointless, self-destructive behavior – not suitable for a middle-aged man like me. I'd had relationships end before, but the sensual excess that had always followed was a failed life pattern I was determined to break.

At first, we kept the breakup a secret, not mentioning it to any of our friends. This eventually turned out to be an important decision, as I will explain later.

A few days after my binge ended, Adam insisted that I go away, and it was true that I did need a change of scenery. So I went to Florida, a place I had enjoyed and where I'd known some degree of happiness. Initially, I stayed in Miami with a friend, who did his best to reintroduce me to the fact that life could be sweet – a thing I could not see at the time. At first, my sense of desperation was such that it almost felt that Adam had died, rather than simply left me. It felt as grief feels, a relentless tug at the heart in which smiling, laughter, were impossible – a pain woven so tightly inside of me that it seemed impossible ever to shake it loose. I would call and text Adam, trying to tell him of my suffering, but he switched off his cell phone to block contact with me. Besides, as noted, I suspected he was by then involved with another man, which would have made my expressions of pain especially unwelcome and intrusive.

I was in a sort of daze by then, unable to believe what Adam was doing to me – in fact, to us. I was so blindsided that I wanted to ask him if he'd really thought through the implications of his actions, if he truly did not think we belonged together, at least enough to try to discuss his apparent dissatisfaction with our shared life. When he did reply to my messages, his heartless tone was more hurtful than the stony silence; he expressed indifference to my feelings, to my sorrow, and to all the possibilities a life together seemed to offer us.

All of this had much more than just an emotional impact. I literally felt that the stress was going to kill me; unable to eat, I lost 18 pounds and began to experience panic attacks. A doctor confirmed that I had had the very chemical balance of my body disrupted in such a way that I couldn't think clearly enough to make routine daily life decisions, nor even to process experiences around me. In my condition, if I'd put my hand down on a hot stove, I might not even have felt it at first.

The doctor recognized that this was not a situation anyone could overcome on their own, and put me on Zoloft, a medication meant to restore that destructive imbalance, and Lorazepam to ward off the panic attacks.

This had all happened so quickly, unexpectedly and with such emotional brutality that it made me revert, by reflex, to the fearful child mode in which I had passed and survived childhood. My nerves were shattered to the point that people would tell me that I was shaking visibly – a condition that has not fully passed away, as of this writing – much as I shook as a child, surrounded by dangers and indifference.

It so happened that Adam's birthday fell while I was still in Miami. Before our breakup, I had intended to decorate our bedroom with balloons, decorations for a night of romance, but by now of course, I was frantic to forget about the day, and the dear friend with whom I was staying did his best to distract me, taking me out partying that day. Unfortunately, as fate would have it, several of the parties seated near us were celebrating birthdays, and seeing all those happy revelers sharpened my memories of the date, and my sense of loss.

Yet I was beginning to heal, even though it was not apparent to me at the time. Perversely, many things in Florida reminded me of Adam. For example, a restaurant near where I was rooming was called, "Adams's Place." And when a local friend took me to visit the home of a friend of his, this stranger's apartment was literally filled with images of Adam and Eve, apparently a hobby of his. Everything around me seemed to force me – cruelly – to think of my Adam.

The very day that I began to grasp how repellent my neediness was, I met a handsome Dominican/Puerto Rican - named Adam- who was madly attracted to me, and with whom I had a marvelous and yet numbed, life-affirming romp.

Having that unexpected and frankly, joyful interlude after so much sorrow, caused me to say to the Universe, "Okay, give it to me. I know you're trying to tell me something, so just give it to me." And I dance to that great anthem of triumphant self-affirmation, Gloria Gaynor's *I Will Survive.*

While I was dealing with immense burdens emotional and physical, it seemed that I might be better off on my own, and so left Pablo's place in Miami to stay at a lovely resort in Fort Lauderdale. It being July, it was low season for such a place in Florida, and Adam, obligingly, paid my travel expenses and hotel bills there.

It took a while to soothe my shock and pain. At first, anger appeared – finally, replacing surprise – in my feelings for Adam, and I started sending him nasty, vengeful messages. I'm not proud of that reaction, but am only human, and was lashing out, reflexively, at the source of my pain – as any injured animal would. But as I started to regain my composure in Fort Lauderdale, it became obvious that the trip to Florida was, in fact, more than restorative; it actually helped my emotional state progress beyond where it had been. Florida was a warm, gentle climate in which life didn't seem to feel like a constant struggle. I started going for long walks, visiting the beach and wading into the calming azure water, savoring my own company.

As I played in the waves, the salty sea water seemed to cleanse me, so that when the sun shone on me, I could feel myself beginning to reflect its brightness like a rough cut diamond. This sensation caused me to grasp that no one – not Adam, not Rafy, not my father - should have so much power over me that I should feel that my own value depended on their love and approval. On those Florida beaches, I realized that I don't need anyone else's help to be a shining gem.

Perhaps more important, I also learned that no one else can prevent me from being such a jewel unless I allow them to do so. If I could still love life after it had shown me so many of its darker aspects, then a diamond – sparkling, indestructible, but the product of terrible forces of pressure and heat on a lump of common carbon - is what Nature seems to have meant me to be.

And reflecting in Florida, I finally realized how needy I still was, texting Adam constantly, grasping for his approval for my every move, hoping he'd somehow snap out of his awful personality shift and take me back. I felt, and deeply believed, that we were so good together that I didn't want us to break up. Now that I realize this, I admire Adam for being so patient with me for so long. He continued to help me financially in Florida while I recovered from being expelled from his life, by which he had nearly killed my spirit.

I should also point out that "the Universe" gave me another form of support during my breakup, and its aftermath – one which I might never otherwise have discovered, but that my crisis summoned forth. At first, Adam and I kept our situation secret from our friends and acquaintances. Not only was I deeply upset, but felt humiliated, not in the least eager to have to talk about the subject to well-meaning people who would surely ask painful questions. But the unexpected help was the gallant and stalwart comfort a few friends gradually gave me – almost literally, "life support."

First honors, and my lifelong gratitude, must go to my friend V She sensed, from disruptions in my routine, that something was grievously wrong. She called me and I told her a little bit. But then it continued and she stood by me and helped pull me out of the sinkhole. Her insistent questions made me pour forth my anguish, which turned out to be the one of the best things I could have done. V was there for me, before, during, and after my time in Florida, a shoulder or (via phone) an ear to cry on anytime I needed it, and a source of wise advice. She never tired of listening to my woes at all hours, multiple times a day.

In this role, V was part of a golden chain of women who have appeared in my life whenever I have most badly needed saving (my grandmother was one, "Dolores's" mother was another, as was my Aunt Nivia). Perhaps this has been Fate's way of compensating me for the absence of the female I should have been most able to depend on for unflinching aid and protection: my mother. In any case, once again, the softness and gentleness of a woman's nature sheltered me against a devastating shock from life.

Another link in this chain of support (though not a female one) was my friend James. After V, he was more helpful than anyone else, but those two were not alone. I late learned that Adam fearing for my safety, had contacted some of our closest friends, told them what had happened, and asked them to reach out to me. I can never sufficiently thank V, James and those others. In my time of thrashing, disorienting need when despair might have destroyed me, they took the role of my phalanx of guardian angels, flying to my rescue when I was feeling especially worthless and unloved.

I had never before realized how very much these good people cared – truly cared – for and about me. It was wonderful – in fact, breathtaking - to see this revelation, especially coming after the horrific surprise of Adam's outburst. They helped preserve my sanity and perhaps my life, providing glittering evidence that there is, beyond question, more to life than disappointment and sorrow – if we will but accept it.

Truly, sometime one must take the sweet with the bitter.

Although I was deeply hurt by the failure of our love for each other, I know Adam and I will be good friends; our lives were simply too intertwined for it to be otherwise. Eventually, his true character must reassert itself, and he will want to undo a great deal of what he has said and done to me. He will read what I write here, realize that it is true, and that he was deceiving himself to adapt a vicious, alien character that is not, and never could be, his true self.

We will never be the couple we once were, but it is a mark of how much I seem to have matured that I can now bear to face that realization. Having said that though, I don't know if I will be able ever to recover completely from such pain – I don't think I'll be able to entirely trust, or love, anyone again after this. I hope that may change, although as of now, having no desire for anyone emotionally or sexually, I am content to let events take their course.

But I started writing this book long before Adam and I split up, long before my respite in Florida, and those awful, and wonderful experiences have only increased my sense of duty to write it, to share some of the very hard-won wisdom of my life with others who may benefit from it. With its help, they may arrive sooner, and less painfully, at the stage of life I sense I am now approaching.

I can pinpoint the exact time when I really and truly said goodbye to being Adam's life partner: July 31st at 8:45 a.m. It was then that I accepted that he had changed so much I no longer had any idea who he actually was.

As noted, one reason this rupture was so devastating was because Adam had made me feel like no one else had in all my connections to other men. To me, this was really like my first authentic, mature, mutually beneficial "love."

But while in Florida, I learned a lot about myself, and was able to figure out things about my latest heartbreak, which would have once taken me many months to grasp. I also realized how well I do when I'm independent; all of this is great progress. Mainly, I recognized that I am very emotionally needy in my relationships (not surprising, given my personal history) in ways that must be noxious to a partner, however loving he may be. And though I believe Adam overreacted and tried to hide his real reason for a breakup (at the advice of some alleged counselor, instead of another man), I can see that his discontent surely arose in large part due to my insatiable appetite for reassurance. So I hereby apologize to him both for my doing that, and for not even noticing it.

This entire experience has taught me that I already have become a lot stronger, and will become even more so. This end of my partnership (and beginning of future friendship) with Adam is simply another chapter in my life, as is creating this book. This is yet another heartache for me, but one whose lesson I may use to help a lot of people I will never meet.

In the course of my life, I have often asked myself, "Why am I going through this? Why do such awful things keep happening to me?" The only answer that seems to offer me hope is that it is not just the random circumstances of arbitrary events, but that it has some purpose behind it.

I believe we are all in this life for a reason, and have come to believe that mine is to show other suffering people that a hopeful heart can always triumph, eventually. My experiences and discoveries can be lessons and encouragement for the many other members of the human race enduring hardships like I have always done.

I make that grand-sounding statement because I think it's fair to say that if I can reach such serenity, given how wretched my life has been in so many ways, it probably means that many people – whose burdens have been less than mine – can get there too.

Arriving back in Chicago, I returned to the apartment I'd shared with Adam, and another shock was in store for me. By this time, I had been gone for more than a month, and our previously immaculate home was an absolute shambles. Adam happened to be there when I arrived, in the process of moving out, and we got into a fierce argument, at first about the mess, but inexorably, about blame for the failure of our relationship.

I had felt very strong and recovered returning from Florida, but the conflict with Adam coming at the very moment of my return, was an immense trial. After he stormed out, still insisting the fault for the failure was all mine, I cried – but then my recovery proved deep, not superficial, and re-asserted itself. I stopped weeping, and cleaned until that filthy apartment sparkled again.

And my Buddhist practice helped save me. I chanted regularly for a month after my return to Chicago, and it helped me fully reach the peace and acceptance I had begun to glimpse – but not fully attain – while in Florida. So, dreadful as the breakup with Adam was, it did lead me, more firmly, back to the practices that have so greatly enhanced my life.

I fully intended to move out of that apartment, with its dense memories of love and happiness, replaced by crushed hopes and dreams. By this time, I had accepted the split from Adam and no longer hoped for or wanted a reconciliation with him – I just wanted to move on to the next stage of my life. But I really wanted to stay in the same Lakeview area, and simply couldn't find anywhere affordable on my tiny SSI income. But in what may yet prove to be a karmic twist of events, one day while I was in the apartment, Adam dropped by. He looked absolutely awful, drawn, dark-eyed and jittery, an appearance that seemed to be the product of both emotional and physical upheaval. After he left, I wept; not out of love, but to see anyone – even one who had hurt me so badly – in such a terrible state.

Adam is a proud, tough, smart man, and when I saw him again shortly after that and told him I could see he was deeply unhappy, he admitted that he absolutely hated where he was currently living. I knew him well enough to get, from that admission, a sense of the underlying problem; he was chafing at being controlled by his new boyfriend. So I took the radical step of suggesting that he move back into our old apartment – with me - but as roommates, no longer as lovers.

At first, Adam refused, but by now, I was far more stable and, actually, in better shape than Adam. So he agreed to return to our old apartment. Adam finally admitted to me, when he moved back in, what I'd long suspected; there was no "counselor" advising him to redress the faults of his relationship with me, he had, in fact, started an affair with another man. For whatever reason, that affair had failed after a relatively short time. Although I no longer loved Adam (in the way I had before), I declined, when he offered to show me a picture of his recent "ex," having no wish to see the instrument of so much misery and heartbreak for me – and now for Adam as well.

In bringing Adam back, I got to do for him what he had done for me, several years earlier, by moving me into his large garden apartment: provide a secure, stable environment, in which he could reclaim his life. I did this out of love – but not out of romantic love, but simply because Adam was a living being in need of help, which, by nature, I provided. And as of this writing, he is beginning to flourish again – as my friend, not my lover.

As I write this, I still expect to have a lot to live, and life keeps presenting me with lessons, challenges, and opportunities, as it does to us all. And – as I am realizing more fully all the time - what I have learned up to this point is serving me well, as a virtuous loop of toughening, softening, and resilience.

In my final chapters, I will try to summarize what, on hard experience and deep reflection, the Universe seems to have been trying to teach me.

"I will eliminate hatred, envy, jealousy, selfishness, and cynicism, by developing love for all humanity, because I know that a negative attitude toward others can never bring me success. I will cause others to believe in me, because I will believe in them, and in myself." Napoleon Hill.

CHAPTER 11

❧

WHEN I THINK ABOUT BUDDHISM, I reflect on how thankful I am. Thankful for finding Buddhism, and thankful for the way it restores my soul. Because it is Buddhist chanting that brought me peace after my split with Adam Just like my friend V did, with her willingness to listen to me share my pain. Just like my friend Pablo did, with his generous offer of a place to stay in Miami so I could heal. To me, Buddhism is like the azure waters of Ft. Lauderdale: gentle, calming, compassionate. Buddhism takes me in its arms and rocks me to sleep.

I find the principles of Buddhism appealing, because they pertain to basic things that humans seek. The principles include happiness, compassion and interconnectedness. It is really so simple. We all want to feel good. We all wish to be treated kindly. We all want to feel like we belong. Buddhism has taught me how to attain these goals. It has also taught me how to reach out into the world with kind, loving fingers, and share the goodness I feel inside.

Buddhism originated in India 2,500 years ago. The teachings derive from those of Shakyamuni, also known as Siddhartha. He aimed to free people from universal suffering. He dedicated his life and his teachings to helping people find spiritual strength.

The teachings of Buddhism are arranged into sutras. One of these, the Lotus Sutra, emphasizes the importance of helping others come to a true understanding of life and achieve what is called the state of Buddhahood. This sutra is the bodhisattva ideal.

Buddhism has always been my beacon, my lighthouse when I was adrift. I had escaped to Florida after my breakup, but the pain returned the moment I arrived back home. I saw Adam, and we had an ugly argument. The confrontation made me realize that I needed something more than a vacation to feel whole again.

The Sunshine State had given me an injection of peace. But Buddhism has provided me with a permanent state of calm. I can return to Buddhism day after day to feel centered and whole.

The tenets of Buddhism revolve around cause and effect. That is, the thoughts I think, and the actions I take, bring about certain outcomes. When my thoughts are filled with joy, I blanket my life with peace and goodness. When I behave in a positive way toward those I love, I guide them to a place of wisdom. I shift the universe to a gentler arc.

Certain actions lead to certain outcomes, because everything is connected. It's all about causality. Thinking angry thoughts and harboring hatred can push good things away. Positivity is life-affirming, but negativity is life-destroying. Behaving in a negative way does not serve anyone. It washes away the good and attracts the bad.

Cause and effect takes place on a personal level. It also occurs on a global scale. And Buddhists seek harmony on a universal level. Buddhism shifts me, my friends, my neighbors and even my enemies from the dark to the light. Buddhism sets sail on a calm sea, and charts a kinder course.

I started looking for that kinder course at age 27. That's when I first chanted with other Buddhists. So I was involved with Buddhism, but then I left for a time. As fate would have it, I was hit by a wave of severe heartbreak and needed a safe harbor.

And so, after my split with Adam, I came back to Buddhism. The ocean lapping at the beaches in Florida had provided a much-needed refuge. But back home, the fast-moving city of Chicago was full of memories of Adam and I quickly noticed I was feeling unmoored again. I needed to feel anchored.

Back home, inside my apartment, despair welled up from deep inside me. My emotions took over my body and mind, and I felt very unstable. I could feel myself spinning down, down, down a rabbit hole.

Buddhism is what cushioned my fall. It gave me a focus, and eased the pain I felt internally. When I began to recite Buddhist chants once more, I felt like I was floating on air. The practice put me on a cloud of peace. It turned my hurt into happiness. It converted my black darkness into white light. In essence, chanting cleansed me.

As I started chanting, I started meeting new people. They invited me to their Buddhist meetings, gatherings and chapters. We chanted together, studied together, ate together. This kept me busy, and made me feel good. I was attracting new friends now -- people with open hearts and strong energy. My spirits improved, and I began to feel good, and I started to forget about Adam little by little, I started to heal.

As I healed, I gained insight, wisdom, and understanding. The more I chanted, the more I felt free. I had felt imprisoned in my troubled mind, but chanting opened the door to that prison. It set me free. So chanting was life-saving for me after the breakup. But not just then. Chanting has saved me throughout my life.

It seems that many people who have an experience similar to mine -- a bad breakup, a divorce, a death -- go through life feeling disheartened. They wonder why difficult things keep happening to them, and why they can't seem to develop effective coping mechanisms.

After a time, these people become angry and bitter. Hatred seeps into their soul. They hurt themselves, or do crazy things that hurt others. They are in such agony that even if they pray, they can't release the pain.

I like practicing Buddhism, because it teaches me how to release the darkness inside. It helps me understand why my life is the way it is, and shows me how to change my karma. Buddhism makes clear that it is preferable to take my pain and turn it into something good.

That is why Buddhism has made me feel reborn. It has shown me that there is, in fact, a bright white light at the end of the tunnel. With Buddhism, I know that no matter what happens, I'll just keep going and going. If one door doesn't open, I push open a different one to make my dream come true.

Buddhism truly inspires me. There are many avenues for me to take, many paths for me to consider. Right now, my focus is on my health and happiness. Because that's what we all crave -- to be happy inside. When we have that, we can navigate life with passion and purpose and fortitude. So that's what I am focusing on at present.

Buddhism is like magic, in a way. Well, it is and it isn't. It is, because through Buddhism, I can converse with the universe and see how I fit in to the master plan. And it isn't, because I am actively involved in shaping my destiny. So nothing is given to me, and yet everything is given to me.

When I earnestly chant for my happiness, or someone else's happiness, things begin to shift. Good things happen, and exciting opportunities reveal themselves. Life unfolds in an amazing way. For some people, it works right away. For others, it takes a while. In my case, Buddhism worked instantly. I felt clear-headed, empowered, strong. So it is clear to me that Buddhism works. My life is the actual proof.

The peace I feel inside is the proof as well. There is nothing better in this world than internal peace. You cannot put a price on it. That is why I am sharing Buddhist practices with other people. I want to show them that they, too, can be happy without material things. No matter how they were raised. No matter if they are jobless, or have served jail time, or were abused, or have gone through any number of emotionally difficult situations.

In my Buddhist gatherings, we teach people to chant "*Nam-myoho-renge-kyo.*" This is so they can be devoted to the mystic law of cause and effect. This thought, and this process, helps them see that they can get along with their children and their neighbors and their family members, and feel happy internally.

And so we rhythmically chant, "*Nam-myoho-renge-kyo, nam-myoho-renge-kyo, nam-myoho-renge-kyo.*" The word "nam" derives from Sanskrit, and means to "dedicate oneself." It is sometimes translated as "take refuge in." But Nichiren Buddhism holds that the natural principle, which governs life in the universe, is present in all people. Therefore, the latter is not the ideal translation.

The phrase "myoho" corresponds to Saddharma, which is the eternal duty, or duty of the soul. The translation of "myoho" is "wonderful or mystic law." It refers to the mysterious parts of our life -- the areas that the mind cannot comprehend. The syllables in "myoho" correspond to life and death, the two aspects of a deeper-life continuum -- one active and manifest, the other latent and unseen.

Nichiren, a 13th century Buddhist monk who lived in Japan, defined "renge" as "cause and effect." He linked it to the lotus flower. The seeds of the flower symbolize how our causes come from the essential realms of life, and how our effects come directly from our thoughts, words and deeds. The pure white blossoms of the lotus flower spring from deep muddy water, illustrating how our highest nature comes from being committed to engaging with the disagreeable realities of life.

Nichiren taught that enlightenment can be achieved by devotion to the Lotus Sutra. The word "kyo" signifies the sutra, or "the teachings of the Buddha." Kyo represents the voice of all living beings. It is the unchanging aspect of the three existences: the past, present and future.

When we put this all together, we get "*nam-myoho-renge-kyo*." Fully translated, this means "dedicated to the mystic law of cause and effect." And so we say this out loud. We chant out loud.

Chanting is a form of meditation. "*Nam-myoho-renge-kyo*" is an energy, and when we chant this phrase, we feel a vibration. We chant this vibration in front of a small shrine, often surrounded by lit candles. The candles lend a peaceful aura to the gathering and to the entire room. Prayer beads, which we hold in our hands, are part of the chanting process too. And before we begin our chant, we ring a Tibetan bowl. We do the same thing after we complete our chant. This gives the chanting session a feeling of circularity and completion.

When I chant, I picture myself feeling the vibration. When I chant, my words and energy go into the shrine, and then come right back to me. By chanting in this way, the chant comes from within me, not outside of me.

When someone does us wrong, we chant for their happiness. But first, we chant for our own happiness. And then something wonderful happens. The chant translates into energy. And then, when we continue the process and chant for the other person's happiness, that chant translates into positive energy for the person we are angry at. It envelops them, no matter where they are. And then things start to happen. Unexpected things. Good things. It's a bit mind-boggling at first. At least that is how it appears to those who are not Buddhists.

Take me and Adam, for example. I began chanting for his happiness, and then continued to do so. Things have turned around, and Adam has been so good to me, and has been helping me, even though he did me wrong. I have been chanting for Adam's happiness for some time now. And little by little, the pain has lessened. Now, even though I occasionally think about what happened between me and Adam, I find that the pain is mostly gone.

In thinking about the breakup, I have come to understand that it is my karma. This is a Buddhist philosophy: we choose in a prior life, what we need to have happen in the next life. So if we are suffering now, it is because of something that happened in our previous life.

In other words, I chose for this situation to happen, I chose the life I've had. We all have. You, me, everyone, we all have chosen these present lives, because of other things we have done in our past lives.

But many people don't understand this concept. That's why they stay so unhappy. If people realized that they could change this -- that they can change their karma through the process and practice of chanting -- they would have the key to finding peace.

Buddhists enjoy sharing this knowledge. We want to introduce other people to Buddhism. We want them to look into it, and try chanting, and attend a local meeting. We want them to learn about the Soka Gakkai International (SGI), and spread the joy of its riches.

And then, once these people benefit from Buddhism, they will want to introduce other people to it. They'll want to help more individuals deal with and overcome their private struggles. So I hope to help people change their karma by chanting. I want them to see that you can go through struggles, like I have, and still be happy.

The word "Buddha" means happy. When we chant, we become happy. We attain Buddhahood. That's why it is a joy for me to be around other Buddhists, because they are naturally happy people. They shine. Regardless of their circumstances, they shine.

I encourage readers to embrace the six core principles of Buddhism: human revolution (inner transformation), wisdom, interconnectedness, compassion, creating value (engaging in life) and treasuring diversity (respecting all cultures). I am publishing my book to help people in this lifetime, and in many lifetimes beyond. That is my goal in sharing my story.

May chanting bring you abundant happiness. May your life shine like mine has.

My Buddhist Altar 2015

"Opinions are the cheapest commodities on earth. Everyone has a flock of opinions ready to be wished upon anyone who will accept them. If you are influenced by "opinions" when you reach DECISIONS, you will not succeed in any undertaking. **Napoleon Hill.**

CHAPTER 12

TO TRY TO PREVENT THE kind of abuse and neglect I personally suffered as a child, I'd like to offer suggestions to any adult readers (especially parents and teachers) charged with the care of young people. This advice is valid for anyone who truly cares about the well-being of helpless, vulnerable little ones. They are based on the many misdeeds and failures of my "guardians" during my youth, acts, which at the time I couldn't realize were morally inexcusable and probably criminally irresponsible.

I pray that most adults reading this are not as apathetic and self-absorbed as were so many of the people who should have been most concerned about raising me - especially my own parents – but including neighbors, teachers, and others who regularly interacted with me.

My mother and father were probably terribly damaged themselves, likely incapable of proper child rearing even if they'd been instructed how. But that is an explanation, not an excuse: There can be *no* excuse for ignoring the fragile treasure of any child's safety and happiness, and that applies (though not equally) to anyone in the child's life, not just those with legal responsibility for him or her. Protecting helpless children from harm is the duty of every decent person. You don't have to disrupt your whole life for it, but if one just turns a blind eye to a child's affliction or doesn't lift a finger, that person forfeits any right to complain about the revolting state of society since he or she isn't helping to improve it.

Warning signs of a child in distress can start at an early age, and recognizing and addressing them promptly can prevent lifetimes of sorrow. Few investments so small in time and effort can yield such pivotal benefits. Being vigilant and willing to help is half the battle, and my advice here may be just the extra help needed to intervene in a child's life before too much pain is inflicted, and permanent damage is done.

First and Foremost Commandment: pay attention to a child's moods.

If he or she often seems ill at ease or unhappy (especially if his or her home or school environment appears stable and nurturing, depending on whether you are the parent, or the child's teacher or school administrator) it very likely means that some problem is happening in that environment that you don't get to see. In my case most, though not all, my problems arose from my home life rather than at school.

Major red flags that something is very wrong in a child's life include an apparently bright child getting bad grades, and/or seeming constantly shy, sad or fearful. But the youngster insists, when asked about such things, that everything is "okay."

I call this response "wearing a veil" and did it a lot myself growing up, hiding the depth of my affliction from adults who, had they known, might have helped me.

I fervently wish some adult in a position to actually deliver me from neglect and physical or emotional abuse had actively investigated why I acted as I did back then, rather than just treating my (out-of-the-ordinary) demeanor as a nuisance. If they had realized I was acting out due to dreadful situations at home and followed up, they might have spared me immeasurable hardship.

And it shouldn't have been terribly hard for the teachers and other adults at my schools to pick up from my behavior and guessed there was something very wrong at my house and done something about it, rather than just let events take their course. They might also have stopped classmates tormenting me for being a "sissy", but did not. As an adult, I know their inaction bordered on criminal negligence. In fact, I now assume some of my teachers must have figured out that my domestic situation was causing my problems, but decided not to complicate their jobs by getting more involved.

So my earlier remarks about the "duty of decent people" to help children in peril apply especially here. They didn't have to adopt me, or challenge my violent father to a fistfight, but they should have done more than nothing; they could at least have alerted official child protection agencies.

So if you detect more than one of the warning signs (poor school performance, or constant anxiety) in a child, he or she is very likely not "okay." Such signs indicate some unseen influence that is preventing him or her from focusing on work at school, or feeling at ease.

And if the child in question protests all is well but you still sense distress, you are almost certainly right - he or she is very probably "wearing a veil." And as soon as no adult is around, he or she will take off the veil (along with any fake smile and false sunny attitude) and shrink back into a bleak dungeon of a life.

Also, notice if the child avoids eye contact, or tries to change the subject when pressed for more information; I did both those things when (as happened occasionally) an adult would ask me how I was during childhood. They are defensive, diversionary tactics, so pay attention for them.

Do not disregard your suspicions. If you detect a veil, don't assume the child is answering freely or rationally – and do not take the easy way out, by accepting such a reply at face value. Don't put words in the child's mouth, but remember, you may have to ask questions that will help him or her effectively express the source of the pain. Probe, but use kindness and sensitivity to cause the child as little (additional) alarm as possible.

Try to remember what it was like to be very young, and how mysterious and baffling the adult world was. A child may not know where to turn for help, what kind of help is needed, and (worst of all – believe me) may fear that he or she may only make matters worse by speaking up.

Children lack the background to recognize or evaluate their options, so it is absolutely vital for concerned (decent) adults to investigate, and if need be, help guide them to rescue.

Before I was fifteen, I was already using a great deal of drugs and liquor, partly because they were common in my environment, but also because they helped blunt the pain of my daily existence, which ranged from mild privation up to lethal danger. Every morning then, I woke up with hatred inside me, thinking ghastly negative things, anticipating a day full of (real or imagined) mistreatment from those around me - and pre-planning retaliatory responses. And I would go to sleep the same way. It was a nightmarish way to have to go through childhood.

But because, as a child, I couldn't know that some of my unhappiness might actually be fixable, I concealed all this – wore the veil - even around people who might have helped me, if they'd known. I was simply too scared and shy to reach out, let alone stand up for myself. Instead, I would take all the anger left from being molested, dressed like a little girl, brutalized and all the other terrors I went through, and try to smother the memories by punishing myself, because not responding - some way, somehow - felt even worse.

I couldn't possibly have explained all that in words then; even now it sounds irrational.

But believe me, it seemed like the only right response at the time.

For example, letting many men penetrate me as a youth offset, for a while, all the emotional pain I felt; they were giving me desperately needed attention (though now I realize they were essentially child molesters). I didn't really know why I was permitting it, but it felt like it was the right thing - in fact, the only thing - to do.

Since it is almost impossible to overstate the importance of spotting a "veil" and looking behind it, I must hammer on that matter some more. A fearful child may, defensively, tell other people what he or she thinks they want to hear, or may be embarrassed to admit to being so helpless. In fact, there were sporadic times in my childhood when adults actually did inquire, with sincere interest, about my well-being. But such curiosity made me reflexively defensive, for the reasons above, so I deflected it.

This happened to me with my dear, kind Aunt Nivia. After I left her house and returned, against my will, to living with my father (her brother), whenever she'd see me she'd ask how I was doing with him, since of course she knew what sort of man he was. But feeling helpless, ashamed and fearing Dad might hear about any criticism and make me even more miserable for it, I dodged her questions.

Years later, I told her how awful my life was at that point. She wept, saying she fervently wished I'd told her the truth, that she could've saved me if she'd known the facts. She still blames herself for believing my false assurances, despite what she knew about my dad – even though she understands how fear silenced me.

So don't rely exclusively on what a child tells you if it conflicts with the evidence. If he or she is visibly upset and failing to thrive, try to be proactive, creative, and inquisitive. Spare yourself the sharp lash of conscience for irreversible failure. Act now: Don't regret later.

Again, don't forget you aren't dealing with someone with an adult's experience or understanding, so pushing too hard can backfire. Don't further upset a child you mean to help by confronting his/her obvious bruises and demanding candor. He or she is scared and confused enough already; to such a child, you may seem to be just one more thing to fear.

If you see the warning signs in a child, probe gently about them. And if you encounter resistance (the veil), just accept that you may simply have to confer with other adults in the child's life. If you must press someone, identify and (discreetly) press people who may be the source of the trouble.

If you sincerely want to help, you must both watch (unobserved, if possible) how the child gets treated by other adults and by other children. You must be prepared to dig, but not to just suddenly undermine even a false sense of security that may be the child's only comfort. If you uncover a problem, offer advice or try to fix it, if it needs adult intervention.

Also, don't rebuke a child for being unable to resolve problems in a way for which his nature isn't suitable, like fending off bullies. If his personality were such that he could fight them off himself, he wouldn't need your help. Helping a child in need is not, invariably, "over-protection."

If you are inclined to chalk up a youngster's apparent misery to a harsh rule that life is hard, be honest with yourself; you too, need outside help sometimes. We all do sometimes, whether it be a physical threat, being swindled by a merchant, cheated by a partner, etc. So if you would call the police to help you prevent or redress a crime, remember, a child too might need help from others. The inclination to benefit others with our strengths and talents is called "civilization."

Again, never forget. Righteous adults must protect children, and if you respond negatively to a cry (or just a visible need) for help, you are failing in that "duty of decency." Worse, the child is apt to just shut down communication with all adults, leaving the unhappiness festering, possibly up to the point of a ruined life.

This brings me to a warning specifically for parents, who bear the greatest responsibility for a child (and who may eventually also get the greatest joy from him or her). A critical part of your work to raise your child is to teach him or her how to interact with the world and to become independent, so caring for them absolutely can't just be a spectator sport.

Always look for signs of shyness, slyness (a survival skill), constant alienation from other children, or a tendency to spend more time with adults than those their own age. It probably means other youngsters tease or bully them constantly. Your child may not be undergoing the truly horrible abuse I did, but that doesn't mean his or her life cannot, and should not, be improved. Persist (without alarming) until you discover the root source of the lack of response.

And even if a child in your orbit shows no overt signs of distress like those noted above, watch how they integrate with life, and with others their own age. One doesn't have to be raped to lose every sense of safety; a child who is getting beaten up occasionally by another child or adult, or who has seen his/her parents go through a bitter divorce can just as easily lose any sense of personal security. Be aware that any major disruptive event can "distort" them; show loving vigilance to ensure such disruptions do as little harm as possible.

Such experiences can linger, and imprint children with a wholly negative view of the world, unless the adults who care for them help. Adults must also explain that while there are many dangers in life, there are almost always good people who will help with problems that seem overwhelming and bewildering to us when we are little - if we just ask. Teach them that they must be careful in life, what kind of people are likely to help (like police), and also that something is terribly wrong if they (the child) must live in constant fear.

To end this chapter on a positive note, I will touch on the incomparable potential rewards of child-rearing, not just its burdens or pitfalls. Parents, in addition to defending your children, build memories with them so that when they grow up, you will have happy shared experiences to talk about, and take pleasure in as a family. Even as a small child, I could tell my father considered me largely just a burden and a nuisance; after all, that's how he treated me. So if that's not how you feel about your children - and if you don't want them to feel that way about you someday - you must show them that, for all the difficulties of parenting, they are still a cherished source of joy and purpose in your lives. Do not assume that a child (especially a frightened one) with no idea how hard adult life is, knows this.

Helping a young person is often a thankless task while it is happening, but can also be one of the greatest senses of accomplishment in anyone's life. It is inherently a long-term goal, a delayed gratification, but can be so very much worth the effort. Just ask any proud mother, father or teacher.

As explained in the previous chapter, my Buddhist practice has helped me find a great deal of the sort of peace and serenity that is, ideally, a part of childhood. But if you want to make sure any children around you – your own, or ones entrusted to your care – don't have a heartbreaking journey through life before finally finding something that can give them repose, you must do so actively.

Because if you don't, who will? Someone already failing at this task?

As I write this, I still expect to have a lot to live, and life keeps presenting me with lessons, challenges, and opportunities, as it does to us all. And – as I am realizing more fully all the time - what I have learned up to this point is serving me well, as a virtuous loop of toughening, softening, and resilience, all at once.

In the next, and final chapter, I will try to summarize what, on hard experience and deep reflection, the Universe seems to be trying to teach me.

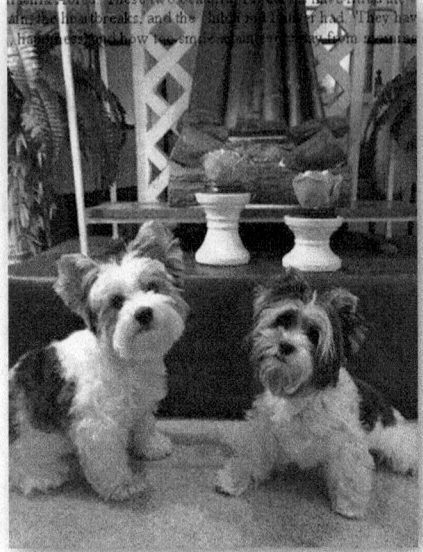

Elvis Abreu and Priscilla Abreu: These two beautiful fur babies have filled the void the emptiness, the darkness, the pain, the heartbreaks, and the childhood I never had. They have brought me sunshine, health, happiness, and how too smile again every day from morning to bedtime.

Everything and everyone in the universe wants to be loved and accepted our personal work is to find the love and acceptance within ourselves. **Shakti Gawain**

CHAPTER 13

❧

IN THIS FINAL CHAPTER OF my book, I will try to summarize what lessons life has seemingly tried to teach me, and which may be useful to others.

Every day, I see many people who are filled with anger and resentment. This leads me to feel that one of the best lessons others might draw from my life story - abandoned in infancy, raped as a toddler by an uncle, raised by and at the mercy of unusually cruel, incompetent adults, is simply gratitude to realize that, by comparison, their own lives have probably been relatively serene. And just knowing a human being can face such challenges and yet endure may give readers hope in the face of daunting circumstances.

Not that mine was the worst possible life, by any means. Many people have, I realize, had even worse trials than my own - a thought that makes me shudder. But I have been told that what makes my story especially affecting is that all my woe has not crushed joy or hope out of me, and threw me into a cauldron of monstrous bitterness, as it might have easily done.

I do not say this out of some sense of perverse superiority or self-pity, but the fact is, most people have not been subjected to sorrows like mine. If you often find life unfair, but such things have never happened to you, please reflect on whether you truly have good reason to waste the precious gift of each day of life in "anger and resentment." Do you really? Or might it just feel empowering to think so?

As I've said in these pages, we must often make choices about how we will approach life: You can let yourself be swallowed, or bestialized, by the dark fight for survival, or you can embrace the light of a world marvelous enough to spawn life and to sustain it. I choose, and have always chosen, to embrace the light.

It seems like hope is what my Karma is directing me to do. And why would I not obey an urge to rejoice, rather than one to seethe indefinitely?

As regards the role of Karma (or Fate, or the Universe): For example, I might never have been born anyplace else other than rural Puerto Rico. That's because, in most places, my mother would have been sent to prison after abandoning her previous child to die. She would never have met my father, and there would have been no me. I choose to read that circumstance as the Universe commanding me into being, and into life - and further, choose to believe it had some purpose for doing so.

Can such things (as my being saved, when my mother's previous child was not) give our lives purpose or even a mission? They can - if we decide to treat them as purposes, or as missions. This is called "agency," meaning taking control of one's own happiness and destiny, at least to the extent any of us truly can.

Life rarely gives definitive answers, solutions that show all other alternatives are wrong. But if my life has not provided "answers," it has certainly offered reasons for hope. Always, in my worst perils and sorrows, help has appeared unexpectedly to rescue me when I needed it most.

Sometimes, it came from people who followed the advice (if only partially) I offered in Chapter 12, about protecting children in danger. Acts like that, which so benefit others (while enriching ourselves) can give real meaning to lives that may otherwise seem pointless.

And of course, I did have some offsetting advantages to all my misfortunes. My grandmother (who saved me after my mother abandoned me to go party, but who died when I was only 5) had a very sunny, easy disposition, according to her son, my gay Uncle Manolin. I probably inherited that nature from her – rather than the sour, aggrieved outlook of my father, her other son – and it may have preserved me. My basically optimistic nature allowed me to outlast the horrors of my youth till I could begin to control the course of my life myself.

My disposition obviously didn't make all my privation and mistreatment easy, but did make it endurable. And we all have both advantages and disadvantages in our lives; it can be reassuring to keep that in mind, at times when only our disadvantages are apparent, and are battering us.

Another strength I had was that I knew what I wanted in life, and didn't let myself be overly distracted to want what society told me I should want. I knew early on that I had a gift and an intense interest for hair care. It wasn't an exalted talent like heart surgery, but that doesn't matter in terms of a satisfying life. My enthusiasm for making other people (and thus, the world) more beautiful was so strong and instinctive. I never really thought about this, it was simply all I wanted to do and it gave me the passion and persistence to do class work needed to obtain a beautician's license in Florida – in record time, and with high scores!

No other goal in my life could have begun to interest me enough to do that, and that achievement shows what one can accomplish by doing what one was meant – and truly loves – to do. Truly, such is the human spirit.

So, dear reader, I might suggest you regard skeptically what others tell you (beyond such duties as providing for a family, which in itself is a reward) about the things you "should" want in life. Would you hate doing what it took to reach those goals? Would doing it fulfill you?

Worse, is it pulling you away from something you feel "propelled" to do as I did, with beauty work?

There was no one to advise me, either way, about what to do with my life, so I just followed my own inclinations. Doing that has not made me rich in money, but has left me deep in contentment, so I have no regrets about following the voices that led me.

Too strong an attachment to the things of this world can be a roadblock to actual happiness. And anger and grudges are among the "things of this world" too; clinging to them is like clasping a burning log, however good the reason to clasp it may seem, it will only prolong the pain to not just let go.

Change and disruption simply go with our being living, sentient creatures. So the question becomes not whether life is inherently good or bad: It is neither, and it is also both. The issue – as noted before – is which do we reach out and grasp? The despair of life's harshness, or the hope of its wonders?

Wildflowers grew outside the perimeter of the Nazi concentration camp at Buchenwald, Germany, where the prisoners could sometimes smell their aroma. Pretty posies couldn't offset the horror of the camp of course, but they did offer reason to feel that even in the face of unimaginable evil, the beauties of life are present, may endure – and may, ultimately, outlast the evil. Most of that camp is gone now, but those flowers still grow where it stood.

My life has been a field of battle between some of the darkest and some of the brightest attributes of the human spirit. Actually, every person's life is like that, if not so vividly. But the dramatic turmoil of mine has given me a hard-won perspective that most people do not have; for that alone, they should be immeasurably glad.

I make no apologies for suggesting lessons some people may find shallow or simplistic. They have kept me alive and even happy; that's good enough for me.

As noted before, I assume my life will go on for some time yet. As of this writing, in mid-2014, at age 53, I have recently had a bout with pneumonia that might have killed me (my HIV status is fairly well-controlled, but still leaves me more vulnerable than most people to illness). But I have since recovered, and continued with my life.

As I have matured, so has my growing awareness that reflections on my life may, if explained and spread, help people who can see no way beyond a sense of life as being essentially without purpose, meaning or value. Every human life has value, and every human can have the purpose or meaning he or she gives it.

But in no case should hope be assumed to be simply, inherently naive. If you seek hope, look for Nature at its most benevolent; and if you need to find that, just look above you on a cloudless day. The blue sky may not always be there – but it will always return.

A birthday gift from the Abreu's and Cruz family thank you guys they know I love the sand and the beach life. Oct . 02, 2013

Always. Know Peace.

Hector A.

www.ingramcontent.com/pod-product-compliance
Lightning Source LLC
LaVergne TN
LVHW021447080426
835509LV00018B/2198